nF420110

*This book is dedicated to all those people
who have suffered or are suffering because
of the misconception that the problem lies
within themselves and not in the
Crooks, Creeps & Bullies (CCBs).
To the Decent Good People (DGPs)
who need to learn that tolerating injustice towards
themselves is not Goodness.*

I hope this book provides you with the strength you seek.

CONTENTS

HANDLING CROOKS CREEPS AND B#$T@*DS

SHIELD YOURSELF FROM THE SHARKS OF THE WORLD

YADHAV MEHRA

Notion Press Media Pvt Ltd.,
No.50, Chettiyar Agaram Main Road,
Vanagaram, Chennai, Tamil Nadu - 600095

Copyright © Yadhav Mehra 2025
All Rights Reserved.

ISBN 979-8-89556-341-0

This book has been published with all efforts taken to make the material error-free after the consent of the author. However, the author and the publisher do not assume and hereby disclaim any liability to any party for any loss, damage, or disruption caused by errors or omissions, whether such errors or omissions result from negligence, accident, or any other cause.

While every effort has been made to avoid any mistake or omission, this publication is being sold on the condition and understanding that neither the author nor the publishers or printers would be liable in any manner to any person by reason of any mistake or omission in this publication or for any action taken or omitted to be taken or advice rendered or accepted on the basis of this work. For any defect in printing or binding the publishers will be liable only to replace the defective copy by another copy of this work then available.

DISCLAIMER

The Oxford Dictionary has many definitions for the word 'bastard'. However, the one the book refers to complies with the following definition:

(Taboo, slang) used to insult (= deliberately offend) somebody, especially a man who has been rude, unpleasant, or cruel.

- *He's a real bastard.*

- *You bastard! You've made her cry.*

- *He's a complete bastard.*

- Your boss is a bit of a bastard, isn't he?

(Source: https://www.oxfordlearnersdictionaries.com/ definition/english/bastard?q=bastard)

Given the nature of the aggressors that have been described, this particular meaning is a fitting tribute to them. In no way are we referring to the other meanings of the word, as defined by Oxford.

Why has this particular word been chosen when there are so many others? It is because it fits the emotion and the sentiment and is a word that is frequently used in common parlance. However, keeping the sentiments of the reader in mind, we have refrained from using it in the later sections of the book and have instead replaced it with the word 'bullies'.

Any offence to any individual, community, or religion is purely unintentional.

PREFACE

I wrote this book because it needed to be written.

When you were growing up, do you ever remember being taught about 'how to handle the vicious in a tough way'? We only learnt about the wise and virtuous and the goodness their deeds rewarded them with. Most of us were never taught by our parents or teachers about the vicious or how to handle them. The moral science classes in schools, the mentoring by our parents, always highlighted the value of virtues. Virtues like tolerance, patience, adapting, adjusting, and compromising were given far greater value as compared to resisting nonsense, braving out the unfair, and calling out the bullies/b#$t@*ds.

I know I speak for my entire generation when I say that it was mind-numbing to constantly focus on the virtues without learning how to handle the vicious. We were supposed to do good, even when the bad ones did bad to us. I remember Gandhiji's popular, oft-parroted dialogue (not sure where and when he said it), "*Yadi koi ek gaal par thapad maare, toh dusra gaal aage kar do.*" (If someone slaps you on one cheek, put the other cheek forward).

This is exactly what was being preached to us. If you get hurt, you respond by presenting them the opportunity to hit you more. This was supposed to make you a 'nice' guy or the 'great' guy, while in reality, it was none of those. It was just a person shying away from conflict.

So, in my view, what was being taught was pseudo-morality and misplaced virtuosity. You are being prepared for compassion, but never for competition, and as much as I would like to say that this would help you, I won't be telling you the truth. While you need compassion in life, you need to be prepared for competition just as much, if not more.

Back in my school days, I was also learning to forgive and forget, but the truth is, I never forgot. I have seen so many people giving and giving and giving, while the person on the other side continued grabbing and grabbing and grabbing. After doing so much 'good', all they got in return was trouble, confusion, and, ultimately, a waste of their time. They lived in the illusion or imagination that someday, they would find the emotional intelligence or emotional stability to stay unaffected by the disparaging behaviour of bad people. They would tell themselves, "I will be *sthitaprajna*[1]. I'll be a man of steady wisdom."

They want to be the tortoise who will withdraw all their *paach indriya* [2]inside, and if people keep hitting on their shell, they will just giggle inside. Their attempt is to strengthen their psyche in a way that they stay unaffected by other people's abusive actions. By doing this, not only are you not confronting the aggressor or aggression, but you are also glorifying tolerating the nonsense. Of course, there is merit in becoming a tortoise (metaphorically

---

[1] Sthitaprajna is a Sanskrit term that means contented, calm and firm in judgment and wisdom. It is a combination of two words: sthita, meaning existing, being and firmly resolved to; and prajna, meaning wise, clever and intelligent.

[2] Pancha means five and Indriya means sensory organ.

speaking); i.e. transcending the impact of the habits of the vicious people to preserve your sanity. This understanding comes with the realisation that fretting and fuming over people's nature leads you nowhere. It is also important to develop the ability to handle the vicious that helps you feel empowered to become a 'tortoise'.

The world considers it disrespectful to disrespect respectful words. The moment you raise your voice against words like tolerance, patience, virtuous—words which have been unquestioningly accepted by society—people roll their sleeves up and curl their fists. I have spoken with almost revolting passion and provided a unique perspective on this subject in my TEDx talk titled: 'Beware Motivational Speakers Ahead'. Standard clichéd wisdom about one-sided virtuosity has become the natural vocabulary of people who do not want people to challenge unfairness.

Every time I hear a person say you should learn tolerance, every fibre of my being wants to speak up against it. Can you imagine telling an abused woman or man to tolerate the abuse they suffer at the hands of their spouse or partner? You think you are glorifying the person's patience and tolerance, but you are just encouraging suppression, repression, and depression, and this will result in a penultimate explosion. After the explosion, the abused person will again go back to tolerating the nonsense and say, "Sorry, I will once again try to be a nice person." It could be anybody from a hysterical husband, a nagging wife, a pestering child, a Shakuni[3] boss, or even a slippery colleague. Unless you learn how to handle these people, you will not find peace by creating some spiritual psychological fog.

My Career has an Intrinsic Role to Play Here

I have done 25 years of extensive training and workshops on subjects which deal with the mind and the thought processes of people. I have coached several different people, and I have learnt that, in the end, all conversations come to one conclusion: 'But he is unfair.'

So, good people will always bring into the conversation the question of, 'How do I tackle that person?' Let me take you through a few more examples:

- How do I tackle that talented, but abrasive person?

- How do I tackle that charming, but unreliable person?

- How do I tackle that servant who steals, but I cannot prove it?

- How do I tackle the driver who surreptitiously looks at my wife or partner through the rear-view mirror?

- How do I tackle people who take advantage of me, but I do not have the courage to confront them?

---

3 Shakuni Mama was the maternal uncle of the Kauravas and the main villain in the Hindu epic, Mahabharata.

You know those books that preach about how you should do the right thing but, in the end, just leave you confused? You are confused about what is the primary right action because there are conflicting values. For example, if leadership is a good value, then followership is also a good value; if justice is a good value, then so is mercy; if fasting is a good value, feasting is one as well.

All of these concerns converged and compelled me to address them by writing this book.

My Confusion was Caused by Several Conflicting Values

'How do I deal with bad people without soiling my soul?'

While justice was a core value, so were harmony and compassion. To fuse all these values together was akin to becoming *decently shameless, wisely selfish,* or *detachedly engaged.* These combo-qualities sounded spectacular but did not help me tackle the vicious people in my life. What it made me realise, however, was that tolerating *adharma* is *adharma* (tolerating unrighteousness is not righteousness). Just because you respect some relationships does not mean they have the right to disrespect you by being wicked or cruel.

I had to raise my voice, take a stand, use tactics, and strategies against intelligently selfish people, or else I would suffer for my entire life. Raising a voice is also important to build a spine, become more real, and lead a life based on one's convictions.

The moment of truth struck when I went through a rough patch with one of my bosses. He was a sharp shark who killed you softly with his power. But, in a way, he was a blessing, as this led me to design a couple of models that would help me and other people combat these uncomfortable situations. Situations that can leave people confused, troubled, tortured, and traumatised at the hands of CCBs (Crooks, Creeps, and Bullies/B#$t@*ds).

These models have helped thousands of people in several countries at several levels, both in their personal and professional lives. People who are caught between goodness and fairness, between personal values and professional goals. People who suffer from misplaced virtuosity and pseudo-morality, which I will touch upon in the next chapter.

The core purpose of this book is to share my practical knowledge with you on how to manage and move along with all categories of people, especially CCBs, so that you can apply it in your daily lives. This book does not mean to place any value judgements on people; it seeks only to educate you on how to deal with people around you to lead a full life.

How will this book help you deal with CCBs? By giving you more clarity on the problem, which will lead to conviction and help you find the courage to become a stronger person and rise above the situation, even though circumstances are against you. Sweet success arrives as we accept our situation/problem, seek a solution, and apply for resolution.

My hope is that the reader shall find their strength with this book. That they understand that there are ways to deal with the selfish-intelligent energies in their lives. These strategies may not be easy to implement, but they will, at least, help you navigate the trying circumstances without questioning yourselves or affecting your morale.

ACKNOWLEDGEMENTS

Bhupendra Soni, my teammate and my rock, for patiently grinning and bearing my endless iterations. Meera, my wife, my biggest 'critic', my travel buddy, and best companion. Her sharp intelligence helped define my concepts of 'misplaced virtuosity' and 'pseudo-morality', and on a lighter side, provided traction, thanks to her willingness to let me test my theories on her. My brother, Raghav Mehra, for supporting my vulnerability, my self-doubting originality, and celebrating the progress during the journey of discovering my authentic self. My father, (Late) Mr Shadilal Mehra, whose immense support can be captured in his one sentence, "Go for it! - always know that I am there for you."

My dog, (Late) Tashi Lama, who tried every trick to disturb me while writing this book, and who eventually, like his name, gave me good luck and buoyancy, let me do my deed for the benefit of society despite his disapproval. My cook, Suresh, who leveraged his culinary craftsmanship and charm, to feed me well and fatten me for the journey. I am also thankful for the immense love, information, and vulnerability that my participants from over 30 countries have showered upon me. To my spiritual teachers for their eye-opening insights, and to the several authors that I have referred to for instilling in me the knowledge and the courage to experiment with various truths.

CHAPTER 1

MISPLACED VIRTUOSITY AND PSEUDO-MORALITY

The world is made up of two kinds of people: DGPs (Decent Good People) and CCBs (Crooks, Creeps, Bullies/B#$t@*ds).

DGPs are good by nature, maybe even without truly understanding the real situation on the ground. They believe in doing the right thing and constantly seek prescribed principles and behaviours that shall help them sail through life. Their principles are primarily borrowed from gurus, books, elders, and blindly followed without examining the context of their own lives. For example, when DGPs try to follow a maxim like 'Forgive and Forget' with a CCB in their life, the maxim works against the DGP.

Haven't we all experienced an unwelcome guest in our house who refuses to leave? Our virtuosity says, 'Atithi Devo Bhava' (Guest is like God), which makes it misplaced.

Misplaced virtuosity is trying to be virtuous in the wrong place, while pseudo-morality is when the lines between morality, legality, and ethicality blur. To clarify, I think legality is the rule of law, *the ruling of the land*; so, in some countries, stoning a person to death might be legal, but is it ethical? Ethics are based on values, beliefs, principles; *what you think is right*. Morality is your scruples, your uprightness on what is sinful and what is virtuous, generally what *religious texts prescribe as right*. I cannot give a clear-cut definition because at some point or another, these mean different things to different people. *It is a matter of perspective.*

I'll explain what I mean: If I say, 'revenge *feels* good', a moral person will most likely lift up his/her hand, distraught, and exclaim "*Nahin* (No)!" While an ethical individual might ponder and say, "*Woh karo jo tumhe theek lage* (Do what you think is right)." And the legal one will hold up the lawful route to say, "*Nahin, yeh hamare desh ka kanoon nahin hai* (No, revenge is not recognised by our law)."

But the real world is very different! What place do words like 'morality' and 'virtuosity' have in it? What do you do if you happen to suffer at the hands of wickedly intelligent people? How do you find relief? Gossiping and backbiting always seem to be the preferred options, but it also creates a toxic environment. When you harbour harmful thoughts towards those who intentionally traumatise you, we allow them to reside in our body and mind, and the toxicity pays rent by creating psychosomatic problems that manifest themselves as mysterious pains or aches. Haven't you heard your friend saying: "This back pain is killing me, but the doctor says nothing's wrong. I got all sorts of scans and tests done, but everything shows up as normal. Then how come I have this pain?"

Now, body aches or other physical ailments can have several biological reasons, but many a time, the reasons are subconscious strain, unconscious stress. When we hold negative thoughts or negative energy in our body towards other people, it toxifies us. It tightens our system and tenses our muscles. As a result, the body loses its synchronicity; the entire musculoskeletal system fails to align with the nervous energy of the body. So, no matter how much your friend exercises, runs, or stretches, the pain remains. Why? Because the negative thoughts are held so tightly that a complete cure is possible only when you sort out your thoughts.

If there are people who cling to toxicity, there are also people who use escapism – the daydreamers who view life with rose-tinted glasses. They keep hoping the bad in their aggressor will change, that they will realise their mistakes and make amends for the better – they've seen it happen in Bollywood movies, after all! This hope subjugates them to continuous degradation from their aggressors. How many times have you let this happen to you? Take a moment to think and reply honestly to yourself.

There are endless examples in our professional and personal lives: siblings taking advantage of each other, difficult in-laws, demanding spouses, manipulative colleagues, and, not to forget, bossy bosses! These people do not play by the rules, and we continue to allow them to inflict wounds upon us. Such situations made me think—was I supposed to live by maxims like 'before you count the mistakes of others, count yours first'? I was always taught to 'look within, look within, look within...'

I think too much of 'look within' can create excessive self-criticism and self-doubt. You are so preoccupied in looking at all the negativity inside you that you ignore the negativity around you. I am not asking you to find fault in others. No, I am asking you to keep a balance. Do not be hard on yourself. This, I can now confidently say, after going through the phase of 'how can I fault others when there are many faults within my personality?' How to face the bad? How to deal with my thoughts? What to do so as to benefit everybody? My mind swayed between looking inside or outside. Should I blame myself or blame others? How much blame could I lay at the other person's door, and how much at my own? Such questions plagued my mind.

1.1 If You Think Self-help Books Will Help, Think Again

To clear my minefield of doubts, I began reading some self-help books. The constant message propagated from the self-help industry seemed to point that the fault was within. You know, be assertive, manage your ontological state of being, candid conversations, cure your thoughts, do breathing, meditation, prayers. It was as Swami Vivekananda said: *Conquer your mind, and you conquer the world.* If you conquer your mind, the wicked will not bother you; again, it's all in the mind.

Do not get me wrong; I respect Swami Vivekananda and am an ardent follower of his teachings, but CCBs are beyond that! Some supportive books suggested conquering the mind through purification practices such as chanting, praying, surrendering, or accepting. Yet other books advised forms of conversations—without any connection with one's psychological and emotional maturity, worship with complete surrender, repetitions of thoughts, visualisations, and assertions—that failed to give long lasting psychological empowerment.

I tried them all. Yes, I did, but nothing worked for me. And I ended up creating a spiritual fog around me. I realised that beyond a point, you can only do so much. I felt that in trying to sort things out just psychologically, spiritually, emotionally, or mentally was akin to blocking the real world. To me, it was pseudo-spirituality, all about suppressing, blocking, internalising, while numerous real-life situations may require venting, releasing, externalising. You cannot sit, chant, or meditate if some rogue attacks you. You need to act. I could not tackle the wicked by my attempts to change my attitude or perceptual lens. At least, I was not one of those who could.

I needed to find a formula, an answer to these questions which would at times tear me apart in terms of what is right and what is wrong. The question for me lay in what is the right action and why do I want to take the right action. *Essentially, I was seeking to be right, not righteous.* It isn't about being politically correct, but wanting to lead a good life upholding values. But the confusion lay in where and how do I apply virtuous values? Justice is a value, as is mercy. Yet, in which situations do you apply justice and where do you apply mercy! Smartness is a value, so is simplicity. Again, I question, which situations call for smartness or simplicity? I was confused as to who is right and what is right, whenever a difference of opinions arose between me and another person. I was perplexed.

I needed to find that formula, a model, a way of thinking that would guide me to peace and prosperity. A solution by which you handle difficult people with the clarity and conviction of doing the right thing. When you are backed by the right values, there is conviction, solidity, a grounding that a person has in their actions. I was looking for the right balance; to speak the truth yet not be hurtful. Anyone can end up with a Shakuni [4]boss, a difficult colleague, a selfish relative, a nagging wife, a pestering child, or a hysterical husband. But on questioning others, I often ended up listening to this Mahabharata story:

One day, Dronacharya[5], the teacher of Pandavas and Kauravas, gives Yudhishthira and Duryodhana a task. Yudhishthira is the good guy, the virtuous. Yet, he does not use his virtuosity objectively or intelligently. He follows the rules, hoping the rules of virtuosity will help him lead a good life. While Duryodhana of Kauravas is a crooked fellow. Now, Dronacharya tells Yudhishthira to travel the world and find a bad person, and Duryodhana is told to seek out a good person. Both bidding their farewells, travel far and

---

[4] The main antagonist in the Hindu epic, Mahabharata, and an extremely intelligent, crafty and devious man.

[5] Dronacharya was a legendary and illustrious teacher of the Mahabharata era, who trained the Pandavas and Kauravas in the art of warfare.

wide. Upon their return, Yudhishthira says, "I could not find any bad." Meanwhile, Duryodhana replies, "I could not find any good." Moral of the story: 'What you think, you perceive.'

Most people are constantly trained to think that if you are spiritual enough, centred enough, your breathing is right, and your thinking is right, and if you are a positive person, then you will find goodness in the badness of others. What you are not trained for is: what if the other person is constantly attacking you viciously, taking you for a ride, and taking the entire credit for all your hard work? What are you supposed to do then? A typical reaction would be one of pseudo-benevolence, to put on a show of indifference and say to others 'what difference does it make', while inside, you are completely crushed...

1.2 What Do You Do When You Face Vicious People?

At some point or other in our lives, we have to confront this question. Some would say, 'give it back'. Some would say, 'No, zip your lip', 'back out', 'lie low', 'don't rock the boat'. A third person would suggest 'compromise, negotiate'. A fourth would say, 'don't worry, God will punish'. A fifth suggestion would be to 'just leave that ecosystem and go away', 'break the relationship', 'move out'. There arises the confusion: What is the right answer? Should we engage or should we disengage? Should we stay or should we leave?

The answer, my friend, lies in one word: context. Contextualise the situation; understand, examine the situation. Context is not just 'what is the problem';

it includes the other person's perspective, your own temperament, and the core problem or intent which needs to be resolved. Running away or turning a blind eye are no solutions. You will have to face the situation; you need to stay in the situation and engage with it. You may still leave the system/situation, but only after you have engaged with it, evolved with it, and learnt something from it. Else, life will keep throwing similar situations at you until you have learnt your lesson. Neither can you run away from crooks, creeps, and bullies, nor can you stay with them, so learn to handle and tackle them!

We are dealing with negativity in people. Once you learn to tackle negativity, the feuding sparks, fireworks, friction, and imbalanced energy in relationships, in any interactions for that matter, will empower you to tackle any situation life may throw at you. Positivity and confidence will fill you once you learn how to deal with negativity. Sometimes, treating the negative can have positive outcomes! *Do remember, you do not become negative once you learn to deal with negativity.*

1.3 Should you confront the wrong, or adapt, adjust, and compromise?

A young boy I met in Decin, Czech Republic answered this question by suggesting that you must stand up for the right. He said, "You may stand to lose, but do not lose your character, your courage, or your conviction." Such experiences only pushed me to explore human nature and their quirks further to find what solution applies where. I was realising personalities and situations have to be further dissected. They have to be, as I keep saying, unbundled, deconstructed, dissected, analysed!

What happens when personalities and values do not match?

Do you resolve it through acceptance, surrender, and unconditional love? There are a lot of similarities between macro and micro; what happens at the country level also occurs at the family level and at the individual level. Say in a nation, one set of people might consider slavery as their right while another set of people in the same nation will disagree. Likewise, within the family, there might be people who will say elders must be respected irrespective of their values—good or bad. While another set of people within the family will say: No, we need to value meritocracy, competence; we need to respect character, not age.

My heart was puzzled when I witnessed intelligent people gypping others. Not paying their share of the resto bill, always taking information but never giving in return, never sharing—basically one-sided relationships. I felt that the more they abused, disused, or misused the world, the more comfortable they were. While the decent ones remained inert, or released their angst by bad-mouthing or gossiping. I could not relate to such living. I was searching for the right way of living.

So, at one end, if the CCBs and their manoeuvrings stumped me, then another set of people at the other end of the spectrum amazed me. I met people who were giving in to calculating, crooked people. These people were no counters, no tit for tat. Life was not a balance sheet for them. They simply gave without expectation. They gave abundantly and harmoniously. The unfairness in the give-and-take ratio did not upset their equilibrium because, strangely, nature squared their accounts.

Whereas here, I was forcibly trying to become tolerant and accepting, while all I was seeking was the right balance between justice and harmony. In my reflections now, I understand these large-hearted givers were not doing a quid pro quo. They were giving consciously or unconsciously, out of choice. It was their nature to nurture. I also saw people around them return their goodness doubly. So, was this also one of the strategies, one of the right ways to live? Do you give if someone tries to grab from you? Do you give if another asks? Or do you selectively say no?

Such large-hearted, generous, not-too-calculating givers rattle me. And my mind tattles: am I supposed to be as large-hearted as them? I wasn't sure if I had such a *vada dil* (big heart)! One thing I was sure of, I wished to live by values of true *dharma*, of being honest to my core.

I have come across intelligent people who can handle CCBs very well, and they are at peace with themselves. Their peace is very real. Their peace is not in the cloud of meditation, breathing, and chanting; shuttered away from the practical world (I have nothing against breathing, meditation, and chanting, and I am sure it works for some people). They are comfortable in the real world, dealing with the good as well as the bad without losing sleep over it.

I realised intelligent people can deal with various shades of grey in people and ably use various strategies. Alas, the same cannot be said for less intelligent or mediocre minds. But a majority of us are middling people. It is difficult for us to deal with CCBs. While some try to escape from problems, some create a spiritual fog around themselves. Yet others oscillate between giving, not giving; being bitter, at times striking, sometimes in silence or even at times with violence. Some of us will be selective to the extent of isolating ourselves, owing to the presence of CCBs. So, in this wide world with so many different people facing complex situations, my quest remained: how do we live rightly?

1.4 Let Me Tell You What Worked for Me

In my pursuit, I found some answers—not based on data or algorithms, but in plentiful experience. I interact and engage a lot with people. I conduct behavioural skills training programmes in the corporate sector— like leadership, self-development, communications, interpersonal, team building, conflict resolution, time management, interviewing skills, even on how to marry right! These life skills are needed to manage one's personal and professional lives.

For example, you need time management in personal life and professional life. You need leadership skills to manage a large, joint family back at home and manage your office team, your community. Yes, interviewing skills are important not only for recruiting suitable people but also for marrying suitably. Besides my sojourns in the corporate corridors, I also coach people individually in highly confidential areas. I am not a clinical psychologist, but I do get an idea of their knocks and shocks, their highs and lows. I get a glimpse into what's bothering them, and I realised that in all these 15-25 years of interactions, countless people wanted to know the answer to one question I myself faced: How to deal with CCBs?

Now, you may or may not be a CCB yourself. You may be a dilution or possess shades of grey. But how do you deal with CCBs, irrespective of you being amongst the good, bad, intelligent, or not so intelligent?

Unlike the epoch of epics where values of justice, truth, compassion, conviction, and courage were highly regarded, these are materialistic times we are living in. There is a shortage of time or resources, desires run high, we are constantly on the run, our nerves are stressed, and stakes are high. In such times, 'how to deal with CCBs' is a message that is required, needed, and wanted by people all over. There are many quotations on 'not to tolerate injustice', but none on how to tackle injustice. I deeply felt the need to chart a way forward to tackle injustice. An actionable map of living unobscured by big ideas.

As the saying goes, 'actions speak louder than words.' So, I began teaching my strategies to deal with the CCBs of the world, and people have benefitted a lot from it.

Some might well ask me, why add another book to the already crowded shelves of self-help books? Let me tell you, all my life when I studied organisational behaviour, organisational psychology, organisational development, pop psychology, self-help books, management books, leadership books, books on interpersonal relations or interpersonal skills—*I found most of these books shied away from shining a spotlight on the 'bad'*. The book would talk about character issues; that's simple – if a person is embezzling funds, you dismiss the person from the organisation. But if a colleague or boss is playing games, is manipulative, what then? How do we engage?

All team models propagate cooperation and trust. Yet, in one-on-one interactions, we discover people have issues; they have problems. The books I have read have shied away from mapping people based on their intent, mapping people based on their character. Why? Because it is not politically correct to label people as crooks, creeps, and bullies formally, while informally, you can even talk behind their backs. Be it in our family or office environment, we do not challenge power equations.

1.5 How Do I Go About Reading or Utilising This Book?

I say, first read the book, enjoy it, feel it, cry with it, and laugh with it. Then pause and think for yourself; hopefully, you will go into a *chintan* (thinking), not *chinta* (worrying), mode! From there onwards, you will journey towards being a *sadhak* (seeker)—eager to experiment, fail at times, partially succeed on other occasions, and sometimes have breakthroughs. You will embark on a fruitful voyage and get better with resisting the wrong and feeling the right. Once you have crossed that threshold, I hope reading this book will deepen your knowledge and give you the conviction and courage to follow your path.

1.6 Who Will This Book Benefit?

The book will benefit anyone from ages 18 to 80 because CCBs and DGPs are a common occurrence across all sectors, segments, classes, masses, psychographics, demographics, geographies, cultures... basically, across all of mankind.

1.7 What You Will Experience When Reading This Book

You may disagree with my theories, or you may agree with the models in the book; you may also feel uncomfortable being confronted with some uncomfortable truths that you have experienced or continue to experience, and you do not wish to be reminded of them.

You may want to read this book slowly, savour each section, pause, and think. Do you relate to what has been written? Does this book empathise with your situation?

Whichever way you choose to read this book, it will be different from what you may have read before on this subject, so be prepared to undergo an emotional rollercoaster. If you are suffering stress at the hands of certain people, this book may actually help you find the courage to stand up and raise your voice. This will not be easy to achieve, but it will help you reach that stage in baby steps. It will make you come to the realisation that the fault is not yours, that you do not need to suffer the oppression. The journey may be difficult, especially if the oppressor is a close family member or friend, or someone whom you love and admire dearly.

And then, of course, at the end of the journey, as you progress, you will experience joy, courage, and freedom. And the conviction to start anew.

CHAPTER 2

THE CCB VS DGP MODEL: WHEN CCBS ARE LESS OR EQUALLY POWERFUL

*C**CB stands for Crooks, Creeps, and Bullies/B#$t@*ds, whereas DGP stands for Decent Good People.*

Think of a story you've read and liked... any story. Or a television series you've seen. What is the one thing that has gripped your undivided attention? Was it the plot, the characters, or the story setting that resonated with you?

What you connected with was the "conflict" in the story. The fight between good and bad, the dilemma between internal beliefs and external situations. Conflict is the heart and soul of every story—be it fiction, non-fiction, or yours!

A famous story consultant once said, "Nothing moves forward in a story except through conflict."[6] What is ironic though is the fact that in real life, we all try to avoid it. Conflict is opposition—it can be internal or external—but we are not here to resolve our internal conflict (I leave that to the self-help books). We are here to resolve the external conflict by resolving our internal conflict—good vs evil, honesty vs dishonesty, truth vs lies, protagonist vs antagonist, DGPs vs CCBs. You might raise

---

6   Robert McKee, the author of *Story: Substance, Structure, Style, and the Principles of Screenwriting*

your eyebrows, but the truth is that we deal with conflict from the day we are born—whether it's the authoritative father, the overprotective mother, the disciplinarian teacher, the demanding spouse, the disrespectful peer, or the bullying boss. The interesting part is that without conflict, we would just be sleepwalking through life. Without conflict, there would be no story.

Before we proceed, let me clarify that I define conflict as differences in thinking and not as an argument or fight between two parties, which is also defined as conflict. If not understood or overcome, though, conflicts can rise to a level of war in our professional or personal lives and can disrupt our mental balance.

Like I said, I call selfish people who grow at the cost of others—crooks, creeps, and bullies/B#$t@*ds—CCBs for short. And if you've chanced upon them, which I'm sure you have, consider yourself lucky. Lucky? Yes, dealing with CCBs empowers you, emboldens you. It's like that Mountain Dew ad—*Dar ke aage jeet hai* (beyond fear lies victory). It fills you with a sense of accomplishment, but more on that later. For now, let's deal with a talented but abrasive team member, crooked friend, creepy relative, or a bullying boss.

You have seen and experienced selfish people, either at work or at home, and you know how they make you feel. CCBs can be demotivating. They make us feel vulnerable, disadvantaged, or inferior. So, how do we deal with CCBs? We can't vent our frustration by beating them up, so we assuage ourselves with watercooler gossip.

This book is about offering a beneficial, long-term solution, and that is: we will learn how to manage them. But just because you are reading this book does not mean that you are sheep being hounded by the big bad wolf! There may be sheep, wolves, or wolves in sheep's clothing amongst us all. So, it's important that you first identify which of these you are and get ready to manage yourself and others.

2.1 People are Complex, Which is Why My Quad 4 I^2 Theory is Simple

Disagreements are a part of life, but contrary to popular opinion, not all conflict situations are bad, no matter how stressful they may seem. Constructive conflict helps us progress, but destructive conflict is debilitating. Essentially, it is the CCBs that cause the utmost discomfort, even to the extent of damaging professional or personal lives.

My years of experience as a corporate trainer and leadership coach have involved innumerable interactions with people of all psychographics and cadres. I have studied and analysed these findings, and this has helped me identify certain behaviour patterns, which I've mapped to specific personality traits. This has helped me create a model, which I've named Quad 4 theory. The theory includes two models designed to help everyone deal with CCBs. One model helps you manage people at a level equivalent to or below you, while the second version helps you manage people with more power and who are in a position higher than you.

These models can be applied to help you manage any kind of CCB, whether they are family, friends, colleagues, bosses, or involve any other kind of social interaction. Before we delve into the theory, I would like to clarify that this is not a one-size-fits-all model. CCBs do not follow a prescribed handbook of behaviours. It is important to also understand and keep the following in mind:

i.   Context is vital.

ii. Character and intent define context.

iii. Intent is measured by TEMP (Time, Effort, Money, Position).

Context is Vital

We love dishing out advice, and why not? It doesn't cost us anything. But before we do this, it is important to first understand the context. Our typical behaviour is such that we listen to people with the intention of replying, and when we have that reply, we stop listening. Let me give you an example: I walk into a corporate class and tell them that in order to climb the ladder, they must work hard. Now, while that may sound like the right advice, it can be completely wrong. If people are overworked and cracking under pressure, this advice could have dire consequences, like physical or mental health issues.

By taking the context into consideration, we can achieve more results. If we truly understand the situation and the nature of the person in question, we can customise our approach. Another important point to remember is that context and the person's state of mind are never static and can be ever-changing.

Character and Intent Define Context

In this model, the two criteria that we use to understand the context are:

- Character

- Intent

Character is a word we are constantly exposed to—*Uska character theek nahi hai* (His character is questionable), *Kya character hai!* (What an unusual person). Character is what comes from within and what defines us as individuals. Character is linked to a person's intent, i.e. What is in his/her heart? In Arabic, intention is called *Niyyah*, and in Hindi, it is *Neeyat*.

Now, a person's character can be either well-intentioned or ill-intentioned. Have you looked at these words closely? The words have character built into their structure. **Well-intentioned** begins with 'We'—which makes the person a 'We' person. A 'We' person has the interests of not just self but also of the others in the ecosystem at heart. On the contrary, Ill-intentioned begins with 'I'—which makes the person an 'I, me, myself' person. It is not wrong to be such a person, but it is highly questionable if it is at the cost of another's well-being and sanity. We simply need to learn how to deal with 'I' people in order for the ecosystem to survive and thrive.

Intent is Measured by TEMP.

How does one identify the well-intentioned or the ill-intentioned? How do we judge intent? The answer is simple. Actions speak louder than words. For actions are the manifestation of intention. I'll simplify it further for you. Observe a person's TEMP utilisation!

TEMP stands for:

- Time

- Effort

- Money

- Position

Notice how a person uses their TIME, where they put their EFFORTS, where they spend their MONEY, and where they put their own POSITION to use. A well-intentioned person uses TEMP for the benefit of 'WE', i.e. 'I, you, us, ours'. They mean to collaborate and ensure that everyone grows – including themselves. And in cases of differences of opinion, which we call here 'conflict situation', they seek an approach that is creative and collaborative. Well-intentioned people will take care of everyone in the ecosystem and not be excessively selfish.

On the other hand, the ill-intentioned direct TEMP for 'I', i.e. for their own benefit. However, I would like to reiterate that there is no judgement in being an 'I' person, unless their rise is at the cost of the people they interact with.

Intelligence Plays a Major Role.

Like character and intent, intelligence is also an equally important criterion for measuring and mapping context. Intelligence indicates how we react to different situations. I have bifurcated intelligence into two types: intelligent and not so intelligent.

The Intelligent:

- Has the sharp ability to discriminate and decipher.

- Is a creature of choice.

- Thinks through situations with a long-term vision, keeping their goals in mind.

The not-so-intelligent:

- Makes decisions based on whims, fancies, impulses.

- Reacts, keeping only short-term goals in mind

- Is a creature of habit.

2.2 Mapping CCBs – The Quad 4 Theory

We now map people based on their character (defined as well-intentioned or ill-intentioned) and intellect (intelligent and not so intelligent). On the X-axis, we place the well-intentioned on one side and the ill-intentioned on the other side. Along the Y-axis, we place the intelligent on top and the not so intelligent at the bottom. Now, we draw two lines through the graph and divide the graph into four quadrants. This gives us the four types of people we are dealing with in a conflict situation (see Fig. 1 © Quad 4 I² Model):

Intelligent	D - Shakuni (CCBs) *Strategy:* Negotiate	A - Krishna *Strategy:* Convince or Get Convinced (C or GC)
Not so Intelligent	C- Duryodhana *Strategy:* Penalty	B - Yudhishthir *Strategy:* *Give from Position of* *Strength for Long enough (GPSL)*
	Ill Intentioned	**Well** Intentioned

Fig. 1 © Quad 4 I² Model

The four quadrants—A, B, C, and D—have been defined keeping character, intent, and intelligence in mind. If we map the people that we have conflict with into these four quadrants, based on their intelligence and intention, it will give us a sense of who we are dealing with and indicate the strategies to confront them effectively and without emotion.

The four categories of people are:

1. The well-intentioned and intelligent,

2. The ill-intentioned and intelligent.

3. The well-intentioned, and not so intelligent

4. The ill-intentioned and not-so-intelligent

If we were to personify these quadrants using characters from the Mahabharata (as this might make them easier to identify), then these would more or less be identified as shown below. However, for the sake of simplicity, we will continue to call them quadrant A, B, C, and D.

Quadrant A is Krishna, the godly charioteer, directing the divine battle.

Quadrant B is Yudhishthira, the good-hearted, but initially weak-minded, Pandava king.

Quadrant C is Duryodhana, the resentful Kaurava, prone to brawls and clashes.

Quadrant D is Shakuni, the darkly scheming uncle of the Kauravas, who craftily alters situations to suit his selfish purposes.

If you've read the Mahabharata, you may have realised that the actual battle was between Krishna and Shakuni, the "Intelligent" ones—the divine fighting the demonic—rather than Kauravas and Pandavas. This is similar to the DGPs fighting the CCBs. Managing the CCB you are dealing with will become easier once you understand their mental make-up, and you can arrive at that by placing them on the QUAD4 graph.

The four quadrants and their role in conflict resolution.

You could end up having conflicts with either one of the four types i.e.:

A. Well-intentioned and intelligent.

B. Well-intentioned and not so intelligent.

C. Ill-intentioned and not so intelligent

D. Ill-intentioned and intelligent.

When you have conflict with Quadrant A - Well-Intentioned and Intelligent

The Strategy to use is - Convince of Get Convinced (C or GC)

Who they are:

- People who truly mean well.

- Their TEMP is directed for the benefit of themselves and for those in their universe.

- They are just, have a sense of reciprocity and promote collaborative growth.

While these people may not be CCBs, there is still a possibility of engaging in conflict with them. In this case, the strategies used for resolving differences with them would substantially differ from the ones you would use with the CCBs. It is important to know and note that conflicts can happen with anyone, even with good people, but that does not make them a CCB. The strategies employed must ensure that the conflict is resolved amicably and without any toxicity or prejudice.

How To Manage Them:

It is best to be upfront with them and place your viewpoint, backed by reason, logic, data, pros, and cons. They are intelligent, which means they have the maturity to handle conflicts and differences.

The strategy that works here is: **Convince or Get Convinced (C or GC)**. In this struggle, meritocracy, reason, logic, and principles will win. This is about rationality, not emotions or ego. Even during conflict, the criticism provided by Quad A is constructive, and this disequilibrium will elevate the relationship between them and the DGP to a higher state of equilibrium. Quad A believe in encouraging their ecosystem; at worst, they will be indifferent, but never demeaning.

When you have conflict with Quadrant B – Well-Intentioned and Not So Intelligent

The Strategy to use is - Giving from a from a Position of Strength for Long Enough (GPSL)

Who they are:

- Not very sharp, cannot discern between bondage and responsibility.

- Abide by social norms and rules, even if others disregard them.

- Are generally compliant, compassionate, and do not retaliate.

Once again, these people may not necessarily be CCBs, but you may still have conflict with them. This may prove to be very frustrating as you may be firing away, but the bullets just keep bouncing off on account of their poor intellect. However, their intention is good, and we do not have to treat them like the CCBs.

How To Manage Them:

The best way to manage Quad B people is to use the strategy of "Giving from a Position of Strength for Long enough" (GPSL). GPSL means you choose to give without any pressure or obligation. It is not a subset of misplaced virtuosity. You give because, innately, it feels right. Giving more than taking is a wonderful way of gaining trust and collaboration with the well-intentioned and not so intelligent. Think of any prominent world leader, and you will realise that this strategy helps them build relationships and stature.

A word of caution though—be sure that the other person is not a taker and is well-intentioned. Generally, for most of us, the GPSL strategy works, but if they expect that you give endlessly and they only continue to take, it signals that the person is not well-intentioned. In this case, GPSL doesn't work; what works is a penalty, which is what we'll discuss next.

When you have a conflict with Quadrant C - Ill-Intentioned and Not So Intelligent

The Strategy to use is - Penalty

Who they are:

- People who are low on intellect, have a poor discriminating faculty, and are creatures of habit.

- Can be petty-minded, selfish, and thick-skinned.

- They enjoy taking and misusing.

It is very difficult to have a discussion with this quadrant. You might be under the impression that such people may come to their senses, realise their unfairness, apologise, and make up for all the damage they have inflicted. They may even manipulate you to believe so. Their nature, *tamsik* (indolent), is programmed or wired to see things as opposite; they see right as wrong and wrong as right. Tricking others is smartness for them, taking from others and not giving back are great deals for them. The strategy of Convince/Get Convinced as in Quad A or GPSL of Quad B does not work with Quad C. Then, how do you handle them?

How To Manage Them:

The only strategy this quadrant understands is loss, that is, if they lose something that is of value to them, especially concerning TEMP (Time, Effort, Money, Position). And that is why the penalty clause is your best defence. Only when their loss is clear to them, can you increase your chances of changing their behaviour. The idea is not to hurt them but cause them pain which they understand and which inconveniences them. It is a direct missive you send which says that if someone hurts you, you will hurt them right back! Quad C doesn't care if they lose their pride or dignity. Their only fear is that they might lose something that's important to them.

When you have a conflict with Quadrant D – Ill-Intentioned and Intelligent – The Main Villains

The Strategy to use is - Negotiate

Now, we come to the most dangerous quadrant, the reason for this book to be written.

Who they are:

- These are "I" people, extremely intelligent and extremely selfish.

- They are discriminative, sharp sharks who will manipulate people and situations for their benefit.

- They grow at the cost of others and utilise their TEMP to suit their own goal.

How To Manage Them:

If you think logic, reason, data—as in the case of Quad A—will help convince them, think again. They will convert, pervert, invert, divert, pollute, dilute all the data that you give to them to suit their needs. They are like slippery fish; whatever angle you throw, they manage to slip out and even rock the boat. Will the strategy of GPSL of Quad B work here? No! That diagnosis will be unhelpful. You will simply be taken for a ride or squeezed dry. The strategy of allowing harsh actions as in the case of Quad C cannot be applied here either, as you are dealing with intelligent individuals, not foolish ones.

What works with Quad D is give-and-take ratios. You have to negotiate with them. They are transactional in a mercenary way and weigh everything against how they will benefit. Quadrant D are highly competitive and treat life as one big competition. Even when you try to negotiate with them, they may remind you of morals, conscience, or duties—basically, invoke your inner goodness to suit their purpose. So, understand their language, competitive mindset, and negotiate—'You do this for me, and I do this for you'. Once again, to clarify, negotiation is a way of life, and there's nothing wrong with it unless it is unfair and manipulative, as in the case of Quad D CCBs.

There are many among us who believe that life is built by relationships, not transactions. There is confusion between *pyaar* (love/affection) and *vyapaar* (business). Remember, with Quad D, it is business. They are transactional. You are making a contract or deal with them. Interact as politely as you can, but adopt a business mindset.

So, that explains the Quad 4 theory. Now that we've understood the four kinds of people we're dealing with, let's understand the two approaches of Quad 4.

2.3 Living Life with CCBs: Two Approaches

There are two ways to lead life while dealing with CCBs.

1. The Inverted U-Way (Clockwise)

Quad C-D-A-B

In this strategy, you start with the assumption that no one can really be trusted. So, you start the interaction by fixing a penalty clause for people who will go back on their word or deal, and that includes a penalty for yourself as well. If none of the parties go back on their word, it negates the need for the penalty, and you can proceed to the Quad D strategy. That is, the penalty clause will be replaced by terms of engagement which clearly specify a fair exchange of give-and-take.

In Quad C, the consequences of not honouring one's word or terms of engagement are very clear, and it is these consequences that compel a person to honour the deal. This means that the level of trust has increased, and while there is no need for a penalty, there are terms of engagement which put it in the realm of business and give-and-take ratios. If this succeeds, then the relationship can graduate to the next level, towards Quad A.

Quad A signifies a maturity in the relationship, which has transitioned from business-like to a level where people are able to engage with logic and reason, and there is mutual respect between parties. Both parties understand that collaboration makes logical sense and that backstabbing is not required, as the parties are familiar with each other, having tried the relationship for long enough.

If the Quad A strategy works, the relationship can move to Quad B. The relationship becomes truly wonderful and symbiotic, especially where problem-solving and stressful interactions are concerned.

2. The Inverted U-Way (Anti-Clockwise)

Quad B-A-D-C

Now, you can begin at Quad B by giving in to CCBs, being the gentleman or lady that you are. With things not working out, you will move to the next quadrant, Quad A, trying to use the language of logic. If things still remain unshakeable, then you use negotiation as in Quad D—do this for me, and I will do this for you. Even if that remains useless, then the only option left is the penalty kick, as per Quad C.

The Way Forward

While I have mapped out the four types of CCBs and their warning signs, this does not mean that you can rush out and apply these principles immediately. As I mentioned, character, context, and intent are important. To know the type of CCB you're dealing with, first study the situation and observe their behaviour over a period of time to understand the strategies they use. Evaluate the situation from their context as well as yours— the reason I say this is because sometimes it is likely that you are at fault.

To give an example, if an employee never submits the assignments on deadline, this can put the other person in a spot. Despite repeated warnings, the employee may not change his behaviour, compelling the other to act in a certain way, which could seem akin to CCB behaviour. Once you've understood the situation, context, behaviour, and other factors, you may have other questions arising. You may even want to debate my theories, which is a good thing, as it shows that you are thinking and not blindly following.

There may be other questions too, like what if a person is a Quad A person in the morning, Quad B in the afternoon, and Quad D in the evenings? Or if the person changes the quadrants depending on the assignment at hand or the person at hand? How will you categorise the person then?

Next, you may want to categorise and map the important people in your life, excluding those that have more power than you. These individuals could be from your family, friends, neighbourhood, anywhere. After mapping them, try to visualise what will happen if you use these strategies with them. Let me warn you, this may not be pleasant, but it is better that you experience this virtually first, as over time, it will fortify you to handle it in real life. If you get lost, confused, or scared at this point, then you may consider attending some of the classes by the author. No-no...this is not a sales pitch but an offer to form a community that helps one another to better themselves with courage and tact.

CHAPTER 3

THE CCB VS DGP MODEL: WHEN CCBS ARE POWER-HUNGRY AND MORE INFLUENTIAL

Which of these statements defines your boss?

- Can't be honest as he/she does not appreciate the truth

- Reprimands me in front of everyone

- Makes me work late every day and even on Sundays

- My boss is pretty understanding

- Insists on work-life balance for the team

- Sanctions leave when I need it

- Gives me full credit for my work

- My boss is my mentor and stands up for me

Quite a few of you, I am sure, have ticked the first few options and are keeping your fingers crossed, hoping that this book will help you convert your boss to a better person. But this book is not about changing them; it is about understanding the CCBs and using strategies to create a better working environment for you, provided you are justified. What do I mean by that?

Well, if you're always pulled up for being late, but you are never punctual, and this affects your work, then your boss is justified. If you change your ways, it may change your boss's behaviour. Remember, the intention matters, and intention cannot be changed by communication; it is changed by productive action.

You will understand the kind of boss you have by his/her intent. How do you handle difficult seniors who are powerful people? This is a complex question, one that can cause great mental trauma. You cannot have a frank conversation. They are not concerned about your career graph. They are in a powerful position that can impede your future prospects.

People Leave Managers, not Companies

A difficult boss is what makes people quit their jobs. A Gallup survey of more than one million people concluded that people don't leave organisations, they leave a bad boss. Surveys quote varying figures of 75-78%, but with the same conclusion. "In spite of how good the job may be, people will quit if the reporting relationship with their seniors is not healthy. *People leave managers, not companies.*" Why does this happen? For several reasons, but primarily because power corrupts.

"If you want to test a man's character, give him power," quotes Abraham Lincoln[7]. The moment a person gets power, he/she is prone to misusing it. If we have to learn upward boss management, then it is important to learn the words and their meanings.

---

[7] Abraham Lincoln was the 16th President of the United States of America from 1861-65. Widely regarded as one of the greatest leaders, he preserved the Union during America's Civil War and abolished slavery.

Who is a boss? Someone who has more power than you. And what is power? Power is an ability or the capacity your senior/manager/supervisor/boss/people have to make you act in a way you do not want to. Thereby, compelling you to do the task.

Once you understand the range of power, you can then suitably respond to stressful situations created by difficult bosses. Whether they simply swivel in their chair and bark orders at you, or keep you on your toes with their camera vision, or take credit for your work, by the end of this book, you will be better 'Boss Managers'!

3.1 The Power Spectrum

I'd like to begin with a disclaimer; we are not boss bashing here. We are simply trying to understand the various types of power and their context. In 1959, social psychologists John French and Bertram Raven studied the power phenomenon and described five power bases.

- Coercive power

- Reward power

- Referent power

- Legitimacy power

- Expertise power.

Six years later, in 1965, Raven added an extra power base: Informational power, i.e. a person's ability to control information, give it, or share it as needed by others to accomplish their work.

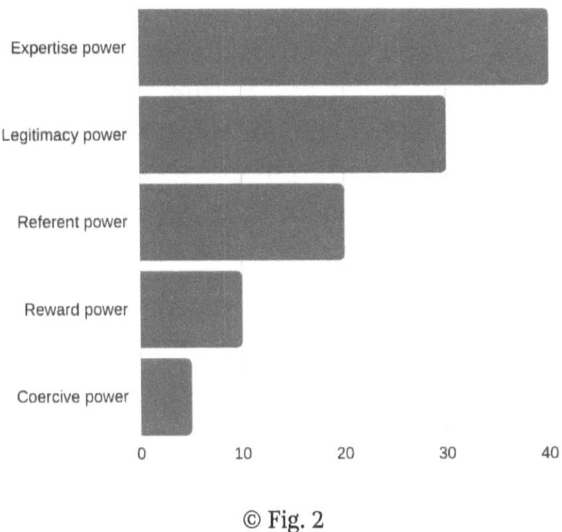

© Fig. 2

Coercive Power: It is the ability or capacity a person has to cause physical, emotional, or economic fear or damage. More like thugs who will barge in and destroy, coercive power uses strong-arm tactics. It implies the use of brute force to physically or psychologically victimise.

It has the bullying ability to scare and force or compel the victim to do the task they want done. It has a vicious, animal-like threat of violence. The victim generally toes the line as his/her physical existence or economic survival is threatened.

Reward Power: This is the ability or capacity to sway people with money, position, or status. It is money power. You do not enjoy what you're doing, but the prospect of a bonus, extra time off, or extra pay keeps you going. Many agree; some happily, some by silencing their inner voice. We've seen so many cases where junior people, on being promoted, mindlessly follow their seniors' commands.

Reward power is slightly higher on the subtle level of compulsion used by powerful people. Money is used as bait. The reward seems alluring enough to follow their manager's orders. Yet, for some, this reward power is disagreeable. Reward power, also, shows its ugly side during the assignment of new projects or signing contracts.

The CCB throws in a sudden googly by adding new requirements or terms, which were not a part of prior discussions. The consulting world refers to this kind of CCB as 'Scope Creep'.

Referent Power: Still higher on the level of subtle compulsion is referent power. It is the ability or capacity to compel another by using one's contacts. It is leveraging the power of connections, contacts, and networks to put pressure on an individual to complete the task.

"I know the PM, CM, DM, GM, and so on. [8]If you don't sanction this email request/order immediately, then I will escalate this to your senior." To avoid hassle, one obeys. Referent power users liberally exploit their connections and drop big names.

Legitimacy Power: Going one level higher than referent power is legitimacy power. Legitimacy power is the power of the chair. It is the ability or capacity to compel others, not because you know people in position, but because you are in that position. You are the PM, CM, DM, GM. You are that company's Managing Director,

---

[8] PM, CM, DM, GM refers to positions of power such as; Prime Minister, Chief Minister, Deputy Manager or District Magistrate, General Manager.

General Manager, or the department's head, an IPS or IAS[9] officer legally authorised to command, to rule.

Legitimacy power is sanctioned by its legal position. Haven't we heard power statements like, "Your appraisal is coming up next month. Do this job, or else I'm not sure what I can do for you"? Terrified of losing livelihoods, many comply. Generally, legitimacy power threatens or guards one's career or professional repute—depending on how you look at it; with power in their hands, one can make or mar others' careers. For sure, because this is one power that all bosses have—the power of the chair.

Often, difficult bosses exploit their referent and legitimate power. They might invert, pervert, dilute, pollute, or mutilate information given to them by their unfavoured employees to present them in a bad light in front of others. For example, the appraisal committee has a list of employee names due for promotion. Now, this committee will exchange notes, and each member will have a different measuring criterion.

We all know, posts are few and candidates many. So, even if one is competent, yet has a disagreeable boss, then his/her chances of making it to the higher post are poof! Not having a supportive spokesperson can impede the employee's chances of promotion.

Expertise Power: This power type is the highest in the power spectrum. Here, knowledge is power. It is the ability or capacity to compel others because you have superior knowledge or skill. The dire need of your

---

[9]   IPS and IAS refers to the two prestigious civil service roles such as; Indian Police Service and Indian Administrative Service.

expertise compels others to surrender to your demands. For example, if you are a heart surgeon with the necessary expertise to perform a complicated surgery, the patient's relatives will do anything you say.

Generally, our bosses have superior knowledge or experience, but there are umpteen cases where the juniors also have more expertise. And countless cases where subordinates use expertise power to benefit themselves. As we have difficult bosses, many times we face difficult juniors too: talented yet abrasive, and equally power-hungry.

They shine at their work, which leads them to exploit their expertise, power, and demand their own pound of flesh from their seniors/managers. For example, a knowledgeable junior accountant in the company, a skilled nanny at home looking after children and ageing parents, or an expert chef behind a restaurant's popularity. They know their worth and need, so you tolerate their pay hike demands or tantrums.

Also, a junior colleague can gain more power than the boss if he/she is better networked. Or, what if your junior team member knows your boss, your superior— then he/she has referent power. Junior colleagues can have expertise power, referent power, or both. Is this the silver lining you were looking for?

Power Does not See Position

Thus, not just powerful superiors but even lesser ranked mortals can easily upset the balance of power. Balance of power is very essential for progress. Power becomes harmful if there is imbalance. Imbalance of power means one person/organisation/country having more power than others.

For example, news in the global political world is full of power see-sawing between the US, Russia or China, which leads us to envision almost doomsday-like scenarios. We need to understand that the imbalance of power emits toxicity, while balance of power brings positivity.

An exception to this is benevolent dictatorship, wherein the head of the state or the organisation exercises absolute power in the interest of the benefit of the population. However, the concept of benevolent dictatorship is also debatable.

Another thing we need to understand: power should be used very sparingly. Sensible people and intelligent bosses use power sparingly in managing people or their juniors. Power is used to influence others, and there are different types of influencing strategies. You have the pull or push-pull strategies to convince others.

Whenever there is disequilibrium or a difference of opinion that needs to be resolved, the best strategy is dialogue. Talk, discuss, converse. In fact, the word 'dialogue' has its roots in Latin, meaning the exchange of logos, i.e., logic. We think logic and reason will work. But in the real world, humans are a bundle of likes, dislikes, whims, and fancies.

People can easily get offended, feel disrespected, or ignored. There is confusion or a thin line between ego (*ahankaar*) and pride (*swabhimaan*). Hence, we need to use a mix of strategies. The pull strategy is a two-way communication, if there is a balanced talk-listen ratio between two people.

While push strategy is one-way communication, it is more or less one person's forceful viewpoint which can create trouble and havoc for others. Alternatively, you push if the other person does not have much to say. What is the best strategy to convince people? I believe that the best influencing strategy to manage people or resolve differences is logic.

Why? Because logic has the least toxicity, while misused power leaves negativity behind. No one likes to be forced to do what they dislike. A good mentor, a sensible boss, or an understanding senior will use power when required but do so sparingly.

Quick Recap

Who is a boss (both in personal and professional life)?

A boss is an individual with power, which comes in various types:

Coercive power: He/she can block someone's regulatory project with fines.

Reward power: Is used money to command authority or block an employee's bonus, pay hikes, promotions, plum projects, or transfers abroad.

Referent power: is used to make others' lives miserable by leveraging their contacts.

Legitimate power: The power of legal authority invested in their position.

Expertise power: Is used not only by seniors but also by juniors.

Our core takeaway is that the balance of power is an essential goal. Perhaps not always easy to attain, but we can always work towards it consciously.

3.2 Unbundling and Deconstructing Boss Management

'Never question the boss. Zip your lip. Buck up. Do not rock the boat. When in the lake, never mess with crocodiles.'

How many of you have heard of or been advised to follow these clichés? All of us, right? Well, THE BOSS IS NOT ALWAYS RIGHT. Sometimes, the boss could be right; sometimes it could be you. At times, both of you could be right, or both of you could be wrong. We spoke about context in the previous chapter—contextualise your thoughts and emotions. Before you react, stop to think and analyse the situation, the person involved, and your own actions or reactions.

Most people ask me, "All this is fine, but how do we handle a difficult boss?"

I reply impishly, "It's a power struggle. Your boss has the power, and you have the struggle! *We do not handle the boss, we tackle power.*"

What do I mean? We all know that the boss has more power than you, but which type of power? To start with, every boss has legitimacy power; it comes with the chair. Your boss can also have additional powers: more expertise power than you, extra referent power, added reward power, and sometimes even coercive power. So, not all bosses are alike.

We will be able to better understand our bosses and their powers after mapping their character and intelligence, just as we did for our colleagues and juniors in the previous chapter.

We place 'character' on the horizontal (x-axis). *Character defined as intent*; **Well**-Intentioned and **Ill**-Intentioned. **Well**-Intentioned are 'me, your, ours', *hum* (we) people. They take care of self and others in the environment. Whereas Ill-Intentioned are 'I, me, myself', selfish people.

It is not a crime to take care of yourself unless it is at the cost of another; it is unfair to the ecosystem. How do we find out one's intent to be *well* or *ill*? We observe a person's actions. *Actions are manifestations of intent.* Note the actions of the person in terms of TEMP—the way they use their TIME, where they put their EFFORTS, where they spend their MONEY, and where they put their POSITION to use.

The logic behind TEMP theory is to figure out how resources are used, be it intellectual, financial, or relational resources. Where does your manager or you invest social capital and intellectual capital? Is it invested for self only? Then, it expresses one's avaricious nature. His/her heart is where the money is!

Take a break and think. Does your boss utilise his/her TEMP to benefit himself, employees, organisation, customers, the entire ecosystem, or does he/she simply use TEMP for self-benefit at the cost of others?

Let us return to the mapping of bosses in detail. Now on the x-axis, we place character—well-intentioned and ill-intentioned, and on the y-axis, we place intelligence. By 'Intelligent', we mean that the person is a creature of choice, does things deliberately, thinks through, has the power to discriminate, to evaluate, and takes action consciously.

But the 'Not So Intelligent' placed in the lower half of the y-axis is more a creature of habit, a person of likes and dislikes, easily affected by offers, whims, and fancies, and almost impulsively reacts to people and situations. After mapping, we get these four quadrants (See © Fig. 3 next page):

- A Well-Intentioned and Intelligent

- B-Well-Intentioned and Not So Intelligent

- C-Ill-Intentioned and Not So Intelligent

- D-Ill-Intentioned and Intelligent

By now, you are knowledgeable enough to detect the 'We' bosses from 'I' ones. Besides, observing 'intent' and 'intelligence', begin applying the power spectrum too in your thoughts. If the person is using money selfishly at the cost of others, then he/she is using 'reward power'. Or if contacting higher-ups or misusing their position for self-interests, then the 'I' person is using 'referent' or 'legitimate power'.

<table>
<tr><td>Intelligent</td><td>D - Shakuni Boss
(CCBs)</td><td>A - Krishna Boss</td></tr>
<tr><td>Not so
Intelligent</td><td>C- Duryodhana Boss</td><td>B - Yudhishthir Boss</td></tr>
<tr><td></td><td>Ill Intentioned</td><td>Well Intentioned</td></tr>
</table>

© Fig. 3

Threatening you with dire consequences? Coercive power is at play. Else, he/she is skilfully influencing others with 'expertise power'. As I mentioned before, power should be used sparingly. Overuse of power over others leads to its corruption and leaves behind toxicity. Remember, a good mentor, a sensible boss, or an understanding senior will use power when required but do so sparingly.

3.3 The Four 'Boss' Quadrants

When asked the question, "Is it possible to manage bosses?"—I clearly say - Yes.

To explain how, let us re-look at the Quad 4 Theory by mapping powerful people/bosses into 4 Quadrants (ref. Fig. 4 © Quad 4 I^2 P Model) based on their intention and intelligence i.e.:

Quad A - Well Intentioned and Intelligent Boss (like Krishna from Mahabharata)

Quad B - Well Intentioned and Not so Intelligent Boss (like Yudhishthir from Mahabharata)

Quad C - Ill Intentioned and Not so Intelligent Boss (like Duryodhana from Mahabharata)

Quad D - Ill Intentioned and Intelligent Boss (like the Sharp Shark Shakuni from Mahabharata)

While the quadrant mapping remains the same as was shown in the last chapter, this time there is a difference - the difference being POWER!

All quadrants of Bosses this time have more POWER than you.

Having mapped different types of powerful people let us start creating strategies for managing them keeping YOUR psychological and emotional maturity in mind.

I'd like to reiterate that the Quad 4 Theory does not support boss bashing. We are simply trying to understand why people behave the way they do and how we can manage the situation (See Fig. 4 © Quad 4 I^2 P Model).

	Ill Intentioned	Well Intentioned
Intelligent	D - Shakuni Boss (CCBs) **Strategy:** 4. Scholars: Act wisely and situationally 3. Fighters: Lobby to fight 2. Traders: Negotiate and encash 1. Followers: Align	A - Krishna Boss **Strategy:** Convince or Get Convinced (C or GC)
Not so Intelligent	C - Duryodhana Boss **Strategy:** Negotiate	B - Yudhishthir Boss **Strategy:** *Take Over and Teach/Do the Right Thing and Share*

Fig. 4 © Quad 4 I^2 P Model

How to handle conflict with Quadrant A Boss/ Powerful person – Well-Intentioned and Intelligent

The Strategy to use is – Convince or Get Convinced (C or GC)

Who they are:

You are one of the lucky ones if your boss is Quad A— Well-Intentioned and Intelligent. They like discussions, ideas, inputs, reasons, and ethics. They love a 'good constructive fight/discussion'. You needn't zip up as you can speak your mind. Use the C or GC—Convince or Get Convinced strategy if there is a difference of opinion, but be sure it is a logical discussion and not a mindless argument, as this quadrant does not suffer fools lightly.

Say, you are working in an investment firm. Your manager directs you to invest money in a particular sector, but you are in favour of another sector. Initially, you may both argue, and tempers may fly, but soon enough, you will be asked to support your reasons with evidence. So, you bring your data and prediction, and he brings his. What will follow is a conducive dialogue where logic, data, meritocracy, principles, and ethics win. In other words, the organisation and the larger cause win.

But a word of caution. Quad A are intelligent, meritorious people. If you are lazy and *kaam-chalao* (easy work) type, you will be at the losing end. They dislike people who take things for granted or have not done their homework, and then argue without any basis just because the boss is open-minded and collaborative.

They respect a 'big fight', provided there is merit and hard work backing the decision. By 'big fight', I mean differences on projects, timelines, pay, or any other subject. They won't waste time if you are not booted up enough.

How To Manage Them:

Whenever you are trying the Convince or Get Convinced strategy with your Krishna like boss, manager or a powerful person, do your homework very well. You must have your data, your spine and boldness to present your case. I stress this point to all; *do not violate the basic norms of polite conversation.*

You must have an internal philosophy by which you live. Bring that to the table. Quad A bosses like it when you ethically stand your ground, backed by intellect. Stick to conversational ethics in terms of the probe/disclosure ratio and in terms of the listen/talk ratio. By which I mean, know how much information you can disclose and how much talking and listening you are allowing for yourself and others.

Always remember, you are having a discussion with a well-intentioned and intelligent person who is looking for good, intelligent inputs from you so that the result of disagreements spearheads a better outcome. Bosses in Quad A respect values such as hard work and detail orientation.

Go in with your case well backed by sound research, data, logic, and empathy. These bosses are looking for higher equilibriums. They want people to challenge them, so never commit the mistake of being 'Yes people' here. Challenge them boldly, but with dignity. They are like Captain Kirk of Star-Trek, "To boldly go where no man has gone before!"

How to handle conflict with Quadrant B Bosses/ Powerful person – Well-Intentioned—Not So Intelligent

The Strategy to use is – Take Over and Teach. Do not Wait. Do the Right Thing and Share.

Who they are:

Quad B bosses are sweet, nice people—well-intentioned but not so intelligent, maybe even less intelligent than you (if you are a Quad A junior). Then, how they became bosses, I'm frequently asked. Well, it's simply because of their age—they joined the company before you. These senior managers are hampered by their own intellect and cannot offer you a great learning curve.

They are not agile enough to create opportunities for growth for you. They may not ably represent your ideas to the management, and neither can they build your brand value. The only saving grace is their intent – they will not use their power to be mean to you, nor will they disrupt your growth out of sheer envy or jealousy.

Quadrant B bosses are not bad, just emotional. Because they have legitimate power over you, they may have volatile outbursts, scream, or get frustrated, but this is purely because of their lack of capacity or capability. They do not have the intelligence to supervise or manage you. So, when differences arise with Quad B bosses, do not wait, just do the right thing.

How To Manage Them:

Let me explain. You cannot look up to Quad B bosses for guidance, because they themselves would be clueless. So, do not wait for their permissions or directions. Use your intellect. If you think a particular situation calls for a certain course of action that is right for the organisation, then go ahead. But keep them in the loop.

Does doing your own thing mean disobedience? I call it 'constructive disobedience'. It is not a bad idea to quietly 'take over'—do the right thing to benefit all. Allow me to share my experience. In one of my earlier jobs as an assistant manager, my manager would direct me to visit the market in a particular inefficient way. My intelligence pointed at the reverse. Of course, he wasn't open to my suggestion, so I quietly followed my own itinerary as I knew the company would benefit from my decision. And it was!

We received big orders, big money, and big celebrations! My boss caught me at the party and said, "You! You did your own thing!"

"Sir, I did keep you informed. I copied you in the mail," was my good boy reply!

"Good for you it turned out well, else—" and he winked. We both ended up toasting to our team and company's success.

Was I lying to him? Perhaps, but it was with good intent and for all concerned. It was more of working silently and letting the results speak for themselves. I will still do it if need be. Sure, your boss will be upset over the insubordination, but the good part of a Quad B boss is that their anger melts when they realise you have taken the right decision, like mine did.

Another strategy that works: 'Constructively confuse' them. Each working day fills our bosses' inbox with hundreds of emails and WhatsApp messages. So, if you decide to follow my strategy and are ever caught for 'constructive insubordination', then simply cover yourselves as I did: "Look, I sent you the email. I cc'd, even bcc'd you, and kept you in the loop."

If they protest further, simply say the client wanted an immediate reply, and the boss was busy. It's all good if the decision has worked in the company's favour! One good thing about Quad B bosses is that you can help them upgrade their knowledge or skills. The other part of this 'Do the Right Thing/Take Over' strategy is to teach/share your knowledge or skills with your boss.

Make a good unison of your intelligence and their good intent, and this collaboration can take you places. Quad B bosses gradually understand that you are more intelligent, and they begin to consult you. The mentor becomes the mentee, and the mentee becomes the mentor. Gradually, in time, they respect you for your expertise, and you respect them for their decency, their niceness, and also their legitimacy.

To quote UG Krishnamurti[10], "Other than learning compassion, it is very important that we teach our children how to handle competition as well." It is a big world out there. You need to arm yourself with as much knowledge and skills as possible to survive, revive, and thrive. Your next two quadrant bosses might not be so accepting or forgiving as the earlier two.

---

[10] Uppaluri Gopala (U.G.) Krishnamurti (1918-2007) was an Indian philosopher who questioned the mystique of enlightenment.

How to handle conflict with Quadrant C Bosses/ Powerful person-Intentioned and Not So Intelligent

The Strategy to use is – Negotiate

Who they are:

Quad C bosses are not so intelligent and ill-intentioned. Your strategy is to negotiate. You need to work out an agreement here. Understand why I say 'negotiate'. The Quad C boss has legitimacy power, plus he/she is selfish and vindictive. Though this doesn't bode too well, yet we assume you are a person with expertise power more than this Quad C boss.

Then, such bosses need you for your expertise power (knowledge) as much as you need them for their legitimacy power (authority). Recall the power spectrum we just read about; you need to bring those powers to the fore to manage Quad C bosses.

How To Manage Them:

For example, your boss has been unkind or mistreating you. Shortly, he needs a presentation to be delivered to the top management. You are the only person in the team to be able to do a stellar job in a short time. He needs you, and you need a breather from him. Politely come to an agreement with your boss—you will prepare the presentation as long as you are given your space. But for this, you have to be delivering top value work.

You need to have more expertise than your Quad C boss. Otherwise, you will need referent power— connections, networking—to manage them. For example, *Mere chachaji aapke boss ko school ke zamane se janate hain*! (My uncle knows your boss since his schooldays.) This may make your boss think twice before coming down heavily on you.

How to handle conflict with Quadrant D Bosses/ Powerful person-Intentioned and Intelligent

The Strategy to use is – As Per Your Inner Core: Followers – Align, Traders – Negotiate, Fighters – Lobby, Scholars – Wisely and Timely Act.

Who they are:

This is the fourth and most difficult quadrant of bosses: Ill-Intentioned and Intelligent. You may require divine help in managing this quadrant, which I call the 'Shakuni[11] quadrant'. Why the Shakuni quadrant? Well, because Shakuni was highly intelligent yet wicked. A sharp shark, swiftly and silently going in for the kill.

Like him, Quad D bosses are extremely selfish and, to top it off, are quick thinkers. Shrewd, clever, and unprincipled, they just know when to hit that sixer and leave you all goggle-eyed. They define the CCB quadrant of bosses: crooks, creeps, and bullies/b#$t@*ds.

If you have a Quad D boss or Shakuni boss, as I did, I sincerely hope my experience helps you. This happened early in my career and what I believe taught me a lesson. I would almost fill up this quadrant in red colour because I learnt it the gory, bloody, gruesome way. How would you feel if you have a manager who is out there to take

---

[11] Famed for being one of the pivotal negative characters of the Hindu epic, the Mahabharata—a villain, who is believed to have veritably changed the landscape of the epic.

away all your hard work, your credit, put you down, use you, and abuse you?

Definitely stifled, stressed, and strung-up. The Gallup survey mentioned that 78% of people leave managers, not companies. Employees leave because the ecosystem is not conducive to their overall growth. Fine, you can choose to resign and look for another job. But if such people occur in various parts of your life—nagging spouses, hysterical in-laws, pestering children, and crooked colleagues—what do you do? You cannot afford to quit in life under any circumstances.

You have to tackle them. Learn to deal with them. How? First, let's ask why many of us have problems. Typically, we would try to work around the trouble areas, but it does not always work. Why? Because we are not sure about our own judgement and lack the conviction required to pick a quadrant and a strategy. Let us understand this further.

Right from our childhood, we hear statements such as, "Look within yourself before you point fingers at others." Nothing wrong with that at all, but despite trying to follow the advice, many of us still lead unfulfilling lives, either personally or professionally. *I think to live fully, it is important to judge people and not be judgemental.* What is the difference between the two?

To judge is to evaluate; it is more neutral and objective, as in a rational or scientific approach. Judgemental, on the other hand, is more or less negative because it can be opinionated, subjective, and generally emotional in nature, with an undertone of a moral, self-righteous approach.

In being judgemental, we bring in a lot of emotions, hatred, one-upmanship, putting down another person to look better. To illustrate, when you say, "He is working hard, doing overtime," you are observing, evaluating, and then judging. You observe and try to describe what you see, hear, or feel. If you say, "He is working hard, doing overtime, just to please the boss," that is being judgemental, as your words indicate a position of self-righteousness.

Being judgemental about people makes us rigid. It is a position of 'I am right, you are wrong'. And such behaviour causes stress in our relationships and prompts us to break away. I am asking you to first observe or collect information regarding your boss's behaviour based on his/her intent.

After evaluation, slot your boss in one of the four quadrants. Then decide your judgement; judge whether your boss is good or bad. Once you understand the difference between judging and being judgemental, it hones your decision-making skills. You decide thoughtfully and fairly, not personally or one-sidedly.

Take this book itself as an example. Only after observing our bosses' character (well-intentioned or ill-intentioned, going by their TEMP use), besides their intelligence, did we evaluate and judge our four boss quadrants.

How To Manage Them:

We've understood how to manage the earlier three quadrants. We now proceed to the fourth, the sharp shark boss, the Shakuni boss. Quad D bosses have more intelligence, better foresight, better decision-making power, good discerning skills, except all of that intelligence is used only to serve his or her purpose.

Armed with awareness, your strategy towards your Quad D boss will depend on your inner nature, your inner core. Psychologically speaking, what kind of a person are you? Are you honest, or are you fine with *sab chalta hai* (accept everything), or does your temper rise quickly, or nothing upsets you? Essentially, how are you psychologically wired? What are your preferences? What are your signature strengths? What comes to you naturally?

Take a break and think about what I am asking of you. This is important. Your inner core decides how to tackle the Shakuni boss. That said, I am sure many of you will jump into self-questioning mode! Be gentle with yourself. As I mentioned earlier, judge yourself or others; do not be judgemental.

3.4 Your Inner Core Decides Your Quadrant D Strategy

Before you understand another, you must first understand your true self, your 'inner core'. The inner core is the sum total of all the values and beliefs that influence our decisions, actions, and behaviour. It is your mental make-up. It is very important to know your inner core because your entire Quad D strategy is going to be based not only on who you are dealing with but also on what it is that you can handle and what it is that you may or may not be able to handle at a later stage.

Based on my experience and learnings, I have created four categories of people based on their mindset, nature, inner core, along with their respective strategies to manage the dreaded Shakuni boss.

1. Followers,

2. Traders,

3. Fighters.

4. Scholars.

1) Followers

These are people who:

- Like to be led rather than lead and are comfortable being a part of another's plan.

- Prefer harmony to fighting, dislike tense atmospheres, and avoid taking unnecessary risks.

- Almost consider it their duty to follow the boss.

- Are relatively passive, submissive, harmony-seeking, and do not want to rock the boat, personally or professionally.

If you are a follower, then your strategy with the Shakuni boss is to align with his intention. By aligning, I mean you are part of the manager's plan. If the boss wants you to do a job, you do it. If the boss wants to take credit for your work, you give it. Plainly put, align means 'be silent and serve from the bottom of your heart'.

Which means that you cannot, and I repeat, cannot make him a part of the lunchroom gossip. Shakuni bosses are sharp sharks, perceptive, and have ears and eyes everywhere. Once they hear that you've gone behind their back, you've lost your loyalty, as they will tear you apart and isolate you.

Follower's Strategy: Despite any misgivings, you align or serve your boss's purpose as the loyalty is rewarding. Hence, you grow along with that person as he/she progresses, for you are an important asset in their talent pool and instrumental to helping them achieve their goal. While followers choose to follow orders as long as they are ethical and do not violate any form of compliance, some may even shut an eye and follow them blindly; the choice is yours.

Though you are reporting to a CCB, he/she has certain requirements from you. You service their requests and don't seek to grab too much credit for it either. But then, how do you benefit? A follower is relational yet understands that the CCB boss is highly transactional. They try to become their boss' real asset, an important cog.

They seek to be indispensable, they do not challenge, and understand the cues pretty well. The follower says, "I give you my alignment, and in return, reward me for my loyalty." Because CCBs are highly transactional, they will aid your growth because they need you, and as they progress, so shall the follower.

After all, the Shakuni boss knows fully well that you are instrumental in executing his plans and strategies in return for a reward. On the other hand, if the follower strategy shocks you and contradicts your inner core, do not worry. You may be another type of person. Let's see which one that is.

2. Traders

These are people who:

- Have mastered the art of negotiation.

- Are naturally good at striking deals and are at ease with the trading language.

- Have a knack for identifying the correct time to strike a deal or request a quid pro quo that will benefit them.

- Work hard for their bosses, but know exactly when to cash in on their efforts and benefit themselves; timing is a key strength.

Trader's Strategy: If you are a 'trader', then your strategy with the Shakuni boss is Negotiate, Transact, Encash the Cheque.

Let me give you an example. My office bought a laptop, and it came with a free digital camera, which nobody seemed to use. The cleaner must've noticed this because one day, he outshone himself in his work. The cherry on the top was the fresh *nimbu* (lime) soda he served my team member, which was to perfection!

So, when the senses were fully elated, he approached my colleague and requested to use the camera for a few days as he was going home. My happy colleague, floating in the blissful cloud of *nimbu (lemon)* soda nirvana[12], agreed! And that was the last we saw of the worker or the camera, as he never returned!

Here's another example. Let's say you've been completing all your work silently for your Shakuni boss. One day, you notice that he returns from lunch in a good mood. The sumptuous lunch, plus the lucrative deal signed, was mind-blowing and has put a smile on his face all day. So, taking that nicely timed cue, you gently approach him and ask him to approve the cost of a course in a prominent university as this will benefit your performance and, thereby, the company.

Being transactional in nature, plus his great good mood, your boss generously takes out his pen and, with a flourish, signs on the form. "Done! *Tu bhi kya yaad rakhega* (You will remember this)."

The trader gives good value, but he also takes it back. He/she has no emotional engagement with the Shakuni boss. The trader employee does not leave the company or manager, but negotiates to ensure a balance of power. The Shakuni boss knows your worth and comprehends your transactional nature too.

They are fully aware and recognise what is going on; you gave something, and now you want something in return. They appreciate that, and they give. By the way,

---

[12]   Nirvana is a place of perfect peace and happiness, like heaven. In Buddhism, nirvana is the highest state that someone can attain, a state of enlightenment, meaning a person's individual desires and suffering go away.

Shakuni bosses do not just dole out crumbs; they can be generous. They give but when they deem fit. Shakuni bosses prefer followers and traders as employees.

You might well ask, "What is the difference between a follower and a trader?" The follower relies on the boss manager to reward him/her. While the trader rewards himself/herself through an advantageous deal; he or she encashes their cheque when the timing and the mood of their Shakuni boss is just right. They are commercially oriented. But if you squirm with qualms at being a *vyapari* (trader) at heart and feel transaction is not your inner core, then read on.

Fighters

This category of people is like warriors.

- Justice is their inner core value; if they see a fight occurring on the road, then 'fighters' are quite likely to jump in to resolve the struggle.

- They do not tolerate injustice, unfairness, and most often find themselves in a warring situation.

Fighter's Strategy: Lobby to Fight with Your Shakuni Boss.

Fighters are more likely to clash head-on with their Shakuni boss. Righteousness is their core, while Shakuni's is deviousness. The fight to set matters right is at the heart of this group of people. They do not wait for decrees but take matters into their hands. Obviously, there will be problems. As with any warrior in any combat, planning is essential.

Warring without any plotting means *khallas* (slaughtered!) Which, in the corporate lexicon, means no promotions, no plum assignments, transfers to some godforsaken place, or even demotions. You do not receive enough stocks. You are not put on the right project or not allotted a good team member. Sometimes, your recruitment or headcount is frozen. You are not given visibility or are snubbed in a meeting or in a town hall." So many consequences.

Which is why, fight only after you lobby. You can fight a Shakuni boss only if you have more expertise or referent power, especially of colleagues, or other top bosses. Hence, lobby. Lobby is a word which is constructively used in America, but not so pleasantly or positively in India.

Lobby is to create your networks, build your own team of people who support you and your ideology. India is lobbying with Australia, Japan, South-East Asia, and America to counter the bullying tactics of China, to give an example. Coincidentally, they too call themselves QUAD!

When you have your own lobby group, your Shakuni boss will not decimate you. For example, what happens when two equally powerful countries seek to conquer? They usually do not confront one another. They might growl or bark at each other, but do not clash. They fight relatively weaker countries.

Similarly, when Shakuni's boss realises there is a lobby rallying for you, they will give you a fair deal. They will not trouble you but will worry others. But if you feel that fighting or lobbying is not your inner core, nor does your nature agree to simply align like a follower or negotiate like a trader, hopefully, the next one is for you.

Scholars

This category of people:

- Are calm, intelligent and well-balanced.
- Kind-hearted by nature and comfortable with the middle path.
- Do not live a life of extremes; do not be excessively temperamental or overly attached.
- Have high emotional intelligence,
- Prefer not to take sudden, extreme decisions.

A scholar is a person of steady wisdom. The Bhagwat Gita describes a scholar as a *Sthitapragnya*[13] someone who is stable and steady.

Scholars Strategy: If you are a scholar, your strategy is to take action wisely and timely-Convince or Get Convinced (C or GC), and for that, align, trade, trade, lobby or fight for the benefit of all, including your Shakuni boss.

Allow me to philosophise a bit. *"Na din, na raat, bas sandhya hi sandhya. Na zyada khana, na kam khana. Na zyada gussa, na kam gussa* (No day or night, only dawn and dusk (the cusp) prevail. No overeating or starving. No high or low anger)!"

Scholars are not aggressive. Being calm and intelligent, they can afford to be appropriate. Appropriateness

---

[13]   Chapter two, verse no. 54 to 72

is a fine balance between courage (*himmat*) and consideration (*tehzeeb*), and scholars walk this fair, thin line with aplomb. Such people are able to speak the truth at the right time, in the right tone (in a neutral tone), for the benefit of all.

They are able to use the 'Convince or Get Convinced' strategy. The Shakuni boss realises he/she is dealing with extremely calm, intelligent, appropriately timed people and gets convinced; in fact, even grudgingly respects them. Take a momentary break here and think of scholars in your life—perhaps a sibling, parent, relative, first teacher, or current boss or team member.

Men and women of steady wisdom possess such high emotional intelligence with sound insight that when tempers run high, they keep quiet, almost seeming as if they are aligning with Shakuni boss. That is not the case.

Their sense of perception is so high that they will not create a conflict when the situation can be resolved without causing disturbance. At times, scholars will act as mediators to negotiate a deal for their Shakuni boss. They will not shy away from saying what they feel is best for the situation, is best for the boss. They do so without violating their inner core or soul.

In managing Shakuni bosses, their wisdom is appropriate, and timing is perfect. They know which strategy to use—whether to align, trade, lobby, or fight. They know when to keep quiet, which battles to fight, which ones to duck, which waves to ride, and which waves to avoid. When the situation calls for it, they may even put their foot down. As a scholar, you will be fairly appropriate, decide on the correctness of the moment, choose which issues to pick, and which ones to let go with your Shakuni boss.

Remember, a scholar does not dither away from the truth. Yet, work progresses without servitude or violence, without sulk or strike. For you are able to look in the eyes of the Shakuni bosses and, in a neutral tone, communicate the heart of the matter. In fact, as I said before, scholars walk a tightrope with Shakuni bosses. It is not easy to walk the thin, fair line of appropriateness for all.

You, as scholars, have to exert far more intellectual and psychological energy to judge a situation while talking to Shakunis. Shakuni bosses themselves, being highly intelligent, realise that when you scholars speak, they need to heed. Scholars speak not just keeping in mind the truth but also the politics of their situation, the benefits, and future consequences.

Which is the best quadrant to be in while dealing with Shakuni boss. It is the quadrant of the scholar—the quadrant of truth, merit, accuracy, logic, reason, and principles. But it is not so easy. Let alone others, even for you or me, it is difficult to behave wisely and timely in each moment of our lives. Some have achieved this feat, but not all. But we all have the objectivity to understand and try our best.

Finally, Practice Your Learning

I would like to share a googly thrown at me during one session. "What if your boss is A in the morning, B in the afternoon, C in the evening, and by late evening, a D boss?" The manager's behaviour keeps changing. At times open and understanding, at times shrewdly intelligent, or at times completely lost. Now, what are you supposed to do?

This stumped me too at first, then I reasoned and answered, "Align yourselves to how the manager is at that time. Do not analyse your boss's personality endlessly. We balance scales of power by handling a person ethically, morally and legally."

Before junior employees deliver judgement about their senior managers, they must understand that they need to work hard and deliver value. Remember, employees have not been hired to pass judgements but to deliver work. The foremost duty (*param dharam*) of any employee is to deliver valued work professionally and ethically. Try to be on a correct professional footing and avoid unpleasant glitches.

My advice: do not get mentally caught up with these four categories (Follower/Trader/Fighter/Scholar). In life, as you move along and gain experience, you could graduate from aligning as a follower to negotiating as a trader. As your negotiating skills improve, along with your knowledge and contacts, you will be able to lobby.

Gradually, you will be able to stand your ground and get better and better at managing Shakunis. In this entire learning process, your inner core remains clean, but you become proficient to handle power, competition, and situations.

Will these strategies work? Yes, one will follow, trade, lobby, or fight to maintain balance of power. I advise you to learn to handle the Shakunis, the CCBs. Understand your situation and know your context, your inner core, your signature strengths, and then move around the quadrants accordingly.

We have observed that when people apply the Quad 4 theory in their work and personal lives, attrition rates go down. They begin to smile at their circumstances and say, "Some days, my boss is in this quadrant, other days here, those days in that one, and these days in this one!" But more on this later.

I have been asked if this is a risky model. Perhaps, I have tried it several times in my life with powerful people. I graduated over the years, sometimes effectively, at times badly, but very often successfully. You have to figure out your path. You might burn your hands, yet keep thinking, practising, and thriving!

We have understood the two models of managing CCBs, and we will deepen our understanding about them by delving into the root cause. But that is for later. Let us first understand why DGPs behave the way they behave. What makes them so submissive? What prevents them from standing up and raising their voice?

Do they find constraint or comfort with their oppressor? Delving into the mind of the oppressed will give us insights into their own behaviour, as well as that of the CCB. Is the CCB a creation of the DGP?

CHAPTER 4

UNDERSTANDING THE OPPRESSED-DECENT GOOD PEOPLE

4.1 Decent Good People (DGPs)—who are they

Decent Good People. What do you think these people are like? Overtly nice? Ones who put others' needs before themselves? People who maintain decency and courtesy with others, irrespective of the latter's demeanour towards them?

Yes, yes, yes. Yes to them all.

While the concept of Crooks, Creeps, and Bullies/ B#$t@*ds (CCB) is relatively new to you, I am sure you are not oblivious to the existence of Decent Good People (DGP). Like CCBs, these people are everywhere. It could be you, it could be me, and it could be anybody amongst us. What I am trying to say is that DGPs are present in our environment as prolifically as CCBs.

Now, let's get to the real question: Who are they?

The fundamental emotional archetype(s) of every person are shaped between the time of their infancy and toddler stage. After that, the learning and unlearning process continues, but the basics have already been set.

At that time, if a child is not made to feel secure about their feelings or activities, they depend on others for approval to affirm that they are doing well. This marks the genesis of approval-seeking behaviour. What happens henceforth? It sets a pattern; DGPs look for approval for any achievement or any particular activity they do.

DGPs seek approval from people, and these people define what will make them a good boy or a girl. In order to become that good boy or a good girl, they are expected to follow certain patterns, certain paradigms, certain commands, and only if these are adhered to are they classified as 'good'.

At times like these, it becomes extremely difficult for a DGP to discriminate whether they are following these commandments to help build their character or to serve the selfish needs of the so-called 'approver'.

This prompts an important question: What is meant by character? Character is the distinct mental and moral qualities that define every individual. It is the sum total of your values. Character is what you are or what you do when no one is watching you. Character is your core.

The first 'approvers' a DGP encounters are usually the parents. Now, they may expect you to be a Satyawan or Savitri[14]; they might even ask you to be a Shravan Kumar[15]. They may drill it into you that if you serve your parents and respect your elders, only then are you a good person. Now, what if the parent is a 'Dhritrashtra'[16]? I do not mean to be disrespectful towards elders. I only

---

[14] A legendary couple in Hinduism known for their love and devotion to each other.

[15] A character from the epic Ramayana, known for his devotion to his blind parents.

[16] A king in the Mahabharata.

intend to demonstrate how and when a person learns the concepts of misplaced virtuosity and pseudo-morality, as defined before.

The dependence begins early enough. As a child, a person develops an addiction to being judged as good because when you are good, you get approval. Therefore, you get into the habit of impressing people and making sure your actions never upset anyone, however much they may exploit you.

Bollywood movies and *saas-bahu* (mother in law-daughter in law) serials stand testament to this mindset and, in a way, are responsible for propagating it. How many countless movies or serials have we seen that glorify people who continue to sacrifice their own needs and desires to do good, despite the continuous ill-treatment meted out by people with vested interests.

It puts on a pedestal their unquestioning servitude or slavish mindset, which is always and only rewarded by disappointment. These martyrs are portrayed as DGPs, probably because of their inability to speak up against the discrimination.

Now, let's take the example of an organisation that advocates a certain set of values, such as integrity, hard work, honesty, and courage. These values are what a company upholds and expects employees to follow under all circumstances. In conferences or workshops, speakers tend to glorify these values.

There are awards given for upholding these values. People become so focused on their implementation that they forget to evaluate the worth of these values and their efficacy in a situation. For instance, you may encounter a real-life scenario where a huge deal depends on the client's intention to operate using an approach that could compromise the organisation's integrity.

What now—will you change your tactics? Let's say profitability, integrity, transparency, and efficiency define the organisation manifesto. What does one do in case of a clash? How do you define which to retain and which to drop? Surprisingly enough, there are no books written on this; it is a topic that is swept under the carpet. These are not easy problems to solve.

Whenever a person publishes a thesis, a bill is passed in the parliament, or a company introduces a new product, it undergoes multiple rounds of scrutiny. Every aspect is examined under a microscopic lens. Every pro and con is weighed, favoured, or criticised. Why is the same process not applied in the case of values?

Let us consider the value of transparency, for example. As an employee, could you choose to be absolutely transparent with your most powerful client? It could very easily have detrimental effects on your personal as well as organisational reputation. As heart-wrenching as it is for me to say this today, it is the truth; people defame their contemporaries to climb up the ladder. The very same values, which were designed as a moral compass for organisational behaviour, now become weapons in the hands of manipulators who twist them to get their way.

Suppose you have a guest in your house who is very happy with your hospitality. However, the moment you suggest that the hospitality needs to be reciprocated, they redirect the conversation towards the topic of generosity and praise your large-heartedness. At this point, a decent person will revel in the praise and think, "Yeah, they are right. I do need to be generous here."

So, what happens is that people keep coming up with different manipulation techniques to trap the DGPs and get their own way.

4.2 Understanding Their Psychology

Let me begin with an anecdote. On one of my trips to Mumbai, I had a very interesting conversation with a taxi driver. He had driven in Delhi before he moved to Mumbai, so I asked him, "Which city do you prefer?"

I received a nostalgic reply, "I like Delhi better because there are no rules there. You can get away with anything."

DGPs love rules. They love the comfort rules provide and believe that if they follow them, they can achieve harmony and avoid conflicts. Rules help chart the course to becoming a good person. If the rules are followed stringently, people will not get upset, nor will there be any unexpected surprises.

It will not give anyone an opportunity to point a finger at them and accuse them of doing something wrong because everything has been done by the book. As we have established, decent good people have an inevitable need to be right at all times and not to be judged. Rules provide this cocooned comfort. Sadly, they are mistaken because not everyone is a *bhakt* (devotee) of rules and invariably, if someone breaks them, it could upset the DGP's balance.

DGPs also tend to invest a lot of energy into becoming decent. This process of becoming a decent or a good person may sometimes blinker their vision and prevent them from indulging in a natural trail of thought. Objective thinking is alien to them.

It is very difficult for them to analyse a situation without perceiving their role in it, i.e. to please everybody in this scenario. My research has led me to the finding that DGPs are not fans of thinking. Eh? How is that possible—everyone thinks, is what you must be thinking!

Let me answer this by explaining what this 'thinking' entails. It usually includes knowing what you want and understanding or navigating the dynamics around you to get what you want. The problem that comes with knowing what you want is that you have to work to achieve it, irrespective of the consequences.

But DGPs are not comfortable with ruffling feathers, so unsettling a situation to fulfil what they want is out of the question. Sometimes, it is the outcome of their thoughts that scares them and makes them shy away from thinking. What if what they thought is wrong, and what if people realised that?

They would be ridiculed, made the joke of the community, probably be disrespected. You're probably shrugging and dismissing this thought as you consider this to be irrational, but for a DGP, these are what nightmares are made of. Approvals are oxygen to their survival, and they wouldn't risk cutting off the supply.

Negotiation: Yay or Nay?

To continue the DGP's dilemma about what they have to do in order to get what they want, they believe that decency demands a quiet transaction. In fact, it is not about 'give-and-take' but 'give and get'. Nobody must ask for anything; the opposite party must give voluntarily. It is a formula that is followed by 'Yagya'[17], where you give an 'Ahuti' (an offering) in a 'Havan Kund'[18].

As a result, the fire rises to bless you. In ritualistic terms, it is not a trade between you and God when you pray or organise a puja (prayer ceremony) for them because you give something and you get something. This reciprocity is what DGPs favour. "You be nice to me, and I will be nice to you—there is no need to discuss that. Instead, we can relish, savour, and enjoy this niceness."

Now, the question this give-and-take relationship raises is one of value—whose part holds more value: the one who gives or the one who gets? Whenever the valuation of this trade is not equitable (and it rarely is), conflict arises. Any negotiation threatens to topple this balance as the other party can always undermine the value provided by the DGP.

---

[17]   Worshipping the supreme lord.

[18]   A fire ritual performed for special occasions by a Hindu priest.

To add to their woes, they have to use words like negotiate, fairness, or deals, words which create imbalance and discomfort. Unfortunately, and this may be to compensate for the sense of security they so seek, DGPs believe that the dignity of a person comes from giving rather than taking.

4.3 The Oppressed Attracts the Oppressors

Growing up, every DGP is taught not to find faults in people. They are repeatedly told—in most cases, by the CCB—to look within themselves when they are bullied. The person could try to control you emotionally, psychologically, or even financially, but you would be forced to take a look at yourself and find the fault within yourself.

Whatever happens to you, whatever people do to you, you blame yourself for letting that happen to you. Whenever a CCB makes a move, they are well aware of their next moves to pull the DGP down even further, as they want something from them. In fact, that is their sole intention.

The DGP's sense of misplaced virtuosity and pseudo-morality makes them believe that stooping to that level will make them no different from the CCB, and this dichotomy is what allows people to get under their skin.

Do DGPs willingly allow CCBs to dominate them? Possibly, and here are the reasons why:

- They suffer from self-doubt.

When a DGP doubts themselves, they rely on the opinion of others. Sometimes, the DGP may not have the ability to think very clearly, but the CCB can very clearly see that this person is going through an episode of self-doubt and capitalises on their indecisiveness. Thus, they use this weakness of the DGP against them. They further sow seeds of confusion and doubt in the minds of DGP to flummox them even further.

- They are scared of disharmony.

Disharmony in relationships is truly what DGP nightmares are made of. They know that if they speak up against the abuse, it will lead to conflict which they are incapable of handling.

- They fear losing the benefits they may be receiving.

CCBs have a way of controlling DGPs, and sometimes this could be by creating false dependency. Now, the DGPs are torn between what they should give up; i.e., do they stop the benefits or the false sense of security the CCBs bestow upon them and find their freedom? Or do they continue with the benefits and live with the pressure?

- Fear of losing CCBs.

Taking the above point of dependency further, DGPs fear handling life alone without the CCB. There is also the fear that the person who replaces the CCB may be worse than the current one they are dealing with. A known devil is better than an unknown one. DGPs also fear abandonment or being disliked, and this only strengthens their dependency on the CCB.

4.4 The Dilemma—Self-care or Public Approval

Freedom gives you the power to script a good life. It ensures that your actions and your decisions are independent of others. You cannot live shackled by the beliefs and expectations of society, and unless you shake this off and free yourself from irrational guilt or victimisation, you will never be able to unfurl your true potential. You will not be able to achieve what truly makes you authentic or unique.

Decent good people tend to live the life of 'another'. They could be living the life of their parents, spouse, or children; where do they fit in all of this? I am not trying to imply, in any way, that you are not supposed to live for others. I am not instigating you to choose to be selfish.

There is a big difference between selfishness and self-care because the latter is about being honest to your desires, to your strengths, to your weaknesses, to your resourceful state, or to what you really want. On the other hand, selfishness is a leech or a parasite that compels you to demand from others what you do not have—selfishness is a vice.

If you do not genuinely care for yourself, you will never really be able to experience the true meaning of happiness. If you don't know who you are, then you will live a perfunctory life where all you do is perform so-called social duties. You will try to please other people because that is the closest you can come to identifying yourself.

None of this will help you experience happiness. You will believe that you are doing the right thing and still be taken for a ride, all while you wait for your karmic justice. So, where do people find relief? They gravitate towards pseudo-spirituality in the hope that it will 'open their third eye' and transform them into the minute atoms and molecules that have made us today.

They aim to transcend the human realm, transcend all earthly thoughts, feelings, and emotions. Well, I am really sad to break it to you, but this mumbo-jumbo doesn't really work. You may become detached from all earthly pleasures, but in the process, you will lose the real connection with life.

The next point I am going to make is very important, and I really want you to understand this well. If you consider yourself to be spiritual and someone in the office is harassing you, what do you do? You shut your eyes and begin to imagine that you are in the mountains, think of flowing rivers, and the peaceful environment that surrounds you.

It might even overwhelm you with happiness, but you know what you are really doing, don't you? You are escaping. You have completely disconnected yourself from the real world. When you connect to spirituality, it takes away from reality, where you keep waiting for the magical moments. What do these magical moments entail?

It may mean that someday you will achieve nirvana or detachment. You may be able to see right through the evil and the wicked, but you may choose to let it pass as you may feel that you are above it. What do you want out of this? You want to be rewarded for your morality, but months, years, and decades will pass without any sign of any reward. At the same time, you will slowly start to disconnect yourself from reality, from the desires, needs, thoughts, ideas, and beliefs that make you who you are.

If you don't do the things that give you enjoyment, whether they are hobbies, an activity, or even making a lot of money, then you are not really living a life of truth because these are the things that you are meant to do. If a monkey is not allowed to jump from one branch to another, then it is a stifled life.

If a lion is put in a cage that keeps it from preying on other animals, how can he assume his rightful position as king of the jungle? When you suppress yourself, you suppress your true potential. When you suppress your true potential, you begin to live a false life. In no way am I trying to imply that spirituality is not an important pursuit in life.

True spirituality is achieved through authentic pursuit and reflection. It is a process of going within while you experiment without. You cannot achieve that inner, alive, happy, truthful silence inside you by creating an imaginative world around you. The first step towards spiritual growth is, 'To thine own self be true', which means one has to be true to one's *swadharma* [19]and psychic fingerprint.

Clarity and Courage

There is this one particular thought that I have invested a lot of my time and energy into; what comes first—clarity or courage? A lot of people are of the opinion that clarity comes before courage. If you do not have the clarity or the conviction, then how will you build up the courage? A few believe that courage, what they refer to as instinctive courage, precedes clarity.

If you want to do something, you should proceed with it, unless, of course, it is a criminal offence. And yet, even with courage, people are unable to move forward with their plan. Why? The reason could be a sense of guilt or a kind of false understanding of how their life is supposed to be.

Now, let's talk about another big dilemma a DGP faces. You may have clarity and conviction on the life you want to lead but are not supported by your ecosystem, i.e. your family, friends, or peers. They stop talking to you and punish you with their silence; they become cold towards you, insensitive, and do not acknowledge your presence; they ostracise you and exile you.

This is a big blow as the DGP thrives on oxytocin, the love hormone. Any imbalance in emotion, and the brakes

---

[19]   Swadharma, meaning one's own Dharma, is doing your duty based on your own ability, i.e. basis one's strengths, abilities and weaknesses.

of their coping mechanisms fail, sending them downhill at breakneck speed.

The DGPs' self-doubt makes them rely on other people, probably even CCBs, to prove their self-worth, to reinforce their competence, and assure them of their worthiness. Independence means freedom from the evil clutches of the CCB, but it also brings a set of responsibilities that the DGP is not accustomed to.

To leave behind people, you have to build up your own confidence. You have to be as strong and powerful as you consider the people around you to be. Most importantly, you have to be prepared because it will be a rocky road ahead. Getting this freedom is important because CCBs sap energy and stunt their growth.

However, if you are able to push back intelligently, you will be able to get a life of your own. This will give you *dhriti*[20]. It will give you consistency or a purpose, which tends to get lost very easily. When an important figure in your life is a CCB, they drain your energy by making you lose your entire sense of focus or accumulation or *tapas*[21].

Thus, to answer the question, in the long run, resisting CCBs should give you peace, and it should give you prosperity. More importantly, it gives you a fine balance between the two.

---

[20] Dhṛti or Dhriti or Dhruti, one of the Yamas, means to 'act with determination', 'patience', 'firmness', and refers to 'perseverance'.

[21] Ascetic practice voluntarily carried out to achieve spiritual power or purification.

While our hearts go out to DGPs, this book aims to help them find their voice and the conviction to push back at their oppressor. DGPs, or pseudo-DGPs, can consciously or unconsciously be manipulative. They may, at times, portray themselves as a victim or a martyr to gain pity.

They may resort to such behaviour—by saying things like, "I am sensitive, my niceness is not getting acknowledged"—in order to avoid confronting a situation. This could only further intensify the CCB's attack. So, whether it is a deliberate game being played by a DGP with 'a particular shade of grey', or an innocent attempt to get balm for their wounds, the DGPs must get out of either playing or be seen as playing 'weakling needs help' games.

4.5 Making a Decision—dealing with CCBs

Let's include two scenarios here:

A. The CCB has more power than you.

B. You belong to the same power dynamic, but you are more gullible.

The solution to scenario A is the most straightforward one: stop being around them. Being around them makes you want to prove that you are a good person, and you will continue to do so until you receive their stamp of approval. The problem is, the CCBs will never confirm this because they intend to exploit your weaknesses. Therefore, trying to get them to approve of you is futile and a waste of energy.

For scenario B, the solution is that when you are around them, don't talk too much. If there is nothing to talk about, don't try to make polite conversation. If they try to put you on the defensive by saying that you do not share anything with them anymore, agree with them and move on.

If they try to ask you too many questions that make you feel uncomfortable, channel your nervous energy by turning the gun on them. Ask them about their life and follow it immediately with a missive, 'you don't share much'. The energy will stabilise when you are on an equal wicket.

They may try to attack you again by saying that you're the one who has been travelling, or that you are the one who meets a lot of people. You can definitely get back to them with a witty remark, or you can smile and stay silent.

One important thing DGPs must learn to do is not to look for collaborative energy. And if it is a collaborative venture, then each of the parties must contribute equally to the activity, and that is something that you can never trust a CCB to do. They will change their behaviour towards you according to their will.

One day, they may be in a good mood and make you feel good about yourself; do not take them seriously. Their mood may change any minute. CCBs always hold back their emotions, so do not expect warmth in these relationships. If you have to constantly face them, you have to adapt to this discomfort to become comfortable with it.

They are deliberately malicious. For example, they could tell you, "You're so fat, I think that's why you need to make so much money."

If you want to get back at them, you have to reply with something equally sarcastic. "You are looking thin today. Is your business not going well?"

Thus, it is an attack for an attack. It will create further discomfort, but frankly, what choice do you have? People will advise you against stooping down to their level, but it will be your task to raise the levels because you have to handle the CCB's negative energy.

How much will you run away from them and for how long? Let me give you an example of what it will turn out to be. You want to run away from the CCB you work with. But there is a CCB present in every segment of every community. Thus, after a few days, you find that the place you considered to be your safe haven is also full of CCBs, so you run away again. To your dismay, you reach another place and find another CCB rubbing his hands in glee.

Thus, one day or another, you will have to empower yourself with the knowledge that you are competent and proficient in handling most of these difficult negative energies. Until then, you have to react to an attack with an attack. Slowly, you will see that your energy, or your ability to deal with these energies, is improving.

Don't commit to anything or be under pressure just because they ask you for something or insist that you owe them something. Stop yourself for a moment and understand your position. In a few days, months, or years, you will see that you are no longer uncomfortable in their presence and can confidently deal with these people.

Let me show you a scenario of how things would be if you develop the comfort to deal with them. You are attending a party where the CCB has also been invited. At the party, you do not feel the need to engage with them. There might be some stiff and tight eye contact, but that doesn't make you uncomfortable, nor compel you to be extra gracious to them for the reassurance of approval you used to seek earlier.

Another way to deal with the situation is by simply mingling with other people in the room. Let the CCB see that you do not squirm in their presence and that you are actually having a good time. You no longer feel the need to get too warm or friendly. Just keep it professional. If they ask you something, reply to the point and do not share any further information.

If they ask if you have seen a particular movie, tell them you have or you haven't. If you have, do not go out of your way to describe the movie. The more information you reveal about yourself, the more you are making scope for them to demean, bully, or manipulate you.

If you know a CCB who is a childhood friend or a person who has known you for a pretty long time, they might try to get away with it by saying, 'oh, we're brothers' or 'we are friends'. Do not let their responses or their tactics get to you. Do not let them overwhelm you to a point from where you cannot come back.

Instead, respond with something like, "Yeah, I know we are friends from childhood, but that doesn't give you the right to behave like this with me." So, when they try to make the atmosphere quite tough or tense, you don't have to take it upon yourself to lighten the atmosphere.

CHAPTER 5

UNDERSTANDING THE OPPRESSOR

5.1 Crooks, Creeps and Bullies/B#$t@*DS (CCBs): Who are they?

As Indians, we believe that everything happens for a reason. That reason sets the very foundation of that event and structures the consequent occurrences accordingly. Similarly, nobody is born with a perception of good or bad. We are taught the same as we grow up. Sometimes, we are led by the good examples illustrated by our parents or teachers, and other times, we learn from misdemeanours.

In our childhood, at one point or another, we have come across that one child who would be mean to another, no matter what. It could be anywhere; it could be deciding to leave a classmate out while playing, it could be them refusing to share their food with another on their table, or it could also be making someone the target of their cruel and deliberate pranks.

Now, there is something about pranks that I would like to add. The idea of a prank has always been associated with 'fun', and most of us have seconded that for a long time. We all have pulled a prank on somebody or the other. We try to make sure that the prank is harmless enough to allow the targeted person to join in our laughter.

Sometimes, the prank can affect the victim in a rather distressing manner. This is when it becomes less of a silly prank and more of a cruel act. This is when you can separate a CCB from a non-CCB.

A CCB would pull a prank for the sole sake of their pleasure. They would like to see the other person go down, and it would fill them with delight to see their vile plan affect them. They are not concerned about the other person's feelings—all they care about is themselves.

Now, this is a recurring cycle. Getting bullied is one of the biggest fears of a child, and this fear can either make them submissive or rebellious, or turn them into another bully. This is the turning point in a person's life; do they submit to their fears and become a DGP, or do they tap into their insecurity and become a CCB? Or do they go beyond these quadrants and become a kind *and* courageous person?

The most common scenarios of bullying can be found on school grounds, but it is absolutely not limited to that. A child can also get bullied at home. Like nature, nurture also plays a great role here. The environment at home or our relationship with our parents affects us with more gravity than we realise.

Thus, a person can become a CCB either due to nature, nurture, or both.

5.2 Where do you find CCBs?

We can find them anywhere and everywhere. Scary thought, isn't it? Unless you have been extremely lucky.

In order to find a CCB, all you have to do is deep dive into your personal and professional lives. I guarantee you, if you look close enough, someone will definitely emerge as a crook, creep, or bully.

While DGPs may be stocking up credits on their karma count, they are also the ones most susceptible to CCBs. The latter has antagonised the former for a very long time, and history is testament to that. Unless DGPs find a Quad A, well-intentioned and intelligent person to stand up for or to protect them, history will continue to repeat itself.

When is a DGP Safe?

- If the DGP is Quad A, Well-intentioned, and Intelligent.

- If the DGP is Quad B-Well-intentioned and Not So Intelligent, but has a Quad A-Well-intentioned and Intelligent person backing them up.

The DGP is safe if she/he is well versed in the CCB management strategies discussed in the earlier chapters. Being proficient in executing the strategies can be life saving for them.

I'm sure we have all been victims of CCBs at some point in time. Let's take a moment to rewind to that precise moment and analyse the situation. It will give you a pretty good idea of how frequently CCBs appear in your life and how naturally they assert their dominance over the ones around them. Let's start by answering these three questions—remember, the only way to solve the problem is by being absolutely honest with yourself.

- When did the incident occur?

- Where did it occur?

- How did it arrive at that?

I am sure, by invoking the past, you might have experienced some discomfort. But, as I mentioned before, you must first accept and learn to confront the problem before you strengthen your forces to tackle it.

My CCB is my boss. Help!

If we look at the traditional hierarchical system, chances are that we will find a good percentage of the bosses or the super bosses being a crook, creep, or bully. Of course, there is no denying that there are some bosses who are simply extraordinary, but this book focuses on that later.

Does any of this sound familiar?

- There's a meeting going on. You're presenting your proposal, and as you finish your presentation, another colleague or even a boss jumps in and takes away all the credit.

- You're running a tight schedule in the office. It is late, and you are almost done with your work. One of your colleagues comes to you and groans about the pressure they're under. They request your help with their work, with the promise that they'll repay the favour. You do all the work only to find out that they deliberately wanted an easy way out. Not only that, they look away or walk away every time he/she sees you approaching them.

- There's been a mistake in a quotation sent out on a project that you're a part of. Maybe you know pretty well who the culprit is but decide to stay quiet for the team's sake. While the management tries to resolve it, somebody needs to be blamed. Before you know it, the culprit has blamed it all on you.

This is a prominent pattern across an organisation and can occur at any level. It could be someone higher up the power spectrum, or a peer who is on the same level, or lower than you.

It is natural to assume that CCBs are those who occupy powerful positions. While it's easier for people standing on a podium to brandish their power, they do not necessarily have to be placed in a socially approved or legitimate powerful position.

Each one likes to make their presence felt in different ways. A subordinate can take you for a ride too; of course, their tactics and manipulation strategies would be different, but their motives would remain the same, no matter what. Their aim will always be to demean, discourage, devalue you and take you for a ride.

We are all well aware of gender discrimination at work. While this is a grave issue, do not be blind to the possibility that a male co-worker or a female co-worker could use gender as a lever to manipulate you.

A CCB in your family is even worse

In an organisation, there is at least the possibility of changing teams or changing your jobs. But relatives are something we are stuck with for eternity, whether we like it or not. Like I said, CCBs are not just a side effect of the workplace; they can exist anywhere and everywhere. It could be your loving husband, your sibling, your cousin, your uncle, your mother-in-law, or even your parents.

Here are some scenarios which I'm sure may sound like a scene from your family album:

- A wife tries to control her husband's time, social network, or purse strings.

- A traditional mother-in-law, unhappy with her career-focused daughter-in-law, disguises her unhappiness by delaying her for the office or overburdening her with extra chores.

- An authoritative parent controls their children by not paying heed to what they want and making all decisions for them. They tend to prove their supremacy by constantly lecturing the child, dishing out boring, irrelevant information purely out of their own selfish need for a captive audience. In the process, they exalt their own (according to their opinion) virtues and demean the child.

- A sibling, jealous of another sibling, pulls them down in front of others.

- A child, out of jealousy and contempt, tries to sabotage the reputation of another child in class.

- In the neighbourhood, someone unfairly acquires a parking slot or blocks two slots to park their car.

- A teacher is biased against a particular student and, on being questioned, manipulates the facts to eventually make her superiors believe her.

The moral of the story is that the one with the power has the upper hand. If CCBs are not presented with the opportunity of *getting* the upper hand, they will grab it somehow. CCBs thrive on power and will go to any lengths to achieve it, be it by merit, manipulative strategies, or force.

If the DGP holds the power, the CCB will shamelessly abuse them by being rude or cruel towards them. DGPs are untrained in the art of responding to indecency and selfishness, and to maintain peace and stability within themselves, they hand over the power baton to the CCB.

5.3 Let's look deep into their mind

Power corrupts. Every relationship has a power dynamic, and this differs depending on the relationship. However, a relationship is only able to maintain equilibrium when each contender has an equal say. (How many such relationships do you know that are in equilibrium?) Whereas, CCBs go to any length to make sure that their opinions or decisions hold more weight than their partner's.

Why do they do this? No particular reason. They do it because they *can*! Notice the use of the verb 'can' here. The usage of the word entirely implies the inequitable exertion of power.

- They try to bring other people down due to their own insecurities. At some point in their life, they, too, might have been bullied, and this would have transformed them into an oppressor.

- Seeing their victims wince feeds their megalomaniac soul. Most importantly, they get a kick every time they see them flinch or frown. This can be termed as sadism at its worst.

- Many deliberately choose to become a CCB to stay ahead of the competition. They believe that prioritising their needs over others' and being insensitive about it will help them achieve success. In brief, they uphold the doctrine of Darwin's 'Survival of the Fittest', where they aim to be the fittest of the fittest. They believe that unless they push people around or down, they will not be able to reach the rank they aspire for. They genuinely believe that adopting the behaviour of a CCB will help them become fearless and valiant. It helps them get what they want, and by that logic, they are right.

Let me share a story. My brother, Raghav Mehra, returned from Colombia with an amazing anecdote.

Apparently, Colombians strongly believe in this one maxim: *If I steal a pineapple from your haversack, the fault is not mine. The fault is yours because you showed me the pineapple.*

Therefore, if I trouble you, then that's because I *can* afford to trouble you, but if you *get* troubled, then that's your incompetence or your inability to endure it.

Blame, blame, blame. One of the CCB's attack tactics. Like I explained earlier when I talked about power dynamics, whoever gets more leverage gets the upper hand. That is to say, if I can take you for a ride, you can't stop me from doing that because *I* retain the final say, because *I* am smarter.

They Don't Bother to Change and Why Should They

Name five CCBs you know who have made a genuine attempt to change. Okay, name three. Two? One? If you have known a CCB for a long time, then you would also know that they hardly make any attempt to change. Why is that?

It is human nature to want everyone to thrive, to strive, to become a better person as time passes by. None of this applies to a CCB. Weird, right? No, not really. Let us see why.

- First of all, once they have tasted power, becoming a better person becomes irrelevant, and they train their conscience to stay silent. Before I proceed, let me define what I mean by 'better' in this case. Better means living a life of success—not just professionally but also personally. A life that is filled with respect, love, and trust pouring in from the people in your ecosystem. A life where there is pride that arises from the goodness of your actions and not from ego.

- They get results without putting in hard work. They are comfortable in violating the work ethic, but no one can really say much to them. They play the cards in a way that they can easily escape the blame game.

My 12-year-old niece, Gayatri, and I were having a conversation when I casually slipped in the question, "Do you have any CCBs in your community or in your classroom?"

She paused a little and then continued, "Yes, there are. I have seen many. Many children are bullies. Whenever they are not happy with your success or with what you are doing, they try to pull you down, to show you in a bad light." She paused. Then she looked at me and fired a missive which, to date, shocks me! She said, "Sometimes, this is encouraged by parents as well."

I must admit, I wasn't prepared for this, and coming from a child, it really shook me. I had delved deep into the topic, prepared theories on it, but receiving this kind of feedback from a person who had witnessed something like this only strengthened my theories. On pondering over it further, I realised that parents encourage CCB behaviour in a child under the garb of 'leadership skills'.

Truth is, that's not how it works. Leadership is about leading a team or a group of people, not about making them lose their edge and pulling them down so that others can succeed. I understand that all parents want is to see their child succeed, but honestly, do you think this is the right way to go about it?

Is It Any Surprise That There are so Many CCBs in Top Positions!

Do not get me wrong, I am not generalising here. There are plenty of organisations with bosses who are mindful of the culture of the workplace and who go the extra mile for the welfare of their employees. I am assuming that the reason to place a CCB in a powerful position is to aid the organisation's growth and profitability.

In this cutthroat, competitive world, organisations are under so much pressure that they are left with no choice but to achieve results, whatever the cost may be. To add to the pressure, an individual's future prospects are linked to how much they can deliver, how soon, and the quality of delivery.

Naturally, bosses are expected to drive this growth and (though I do not agree with this), this could inadvertently lead to CCB behaviour. On the flip side, the company might incur more profits, but the workspace experiences a drastic change. Once they are in power, every subordinate suffers at their hands. Their creativity and innovation could be impacted, eventually compelling the employee to hand in his resignation.

So far, we have heard about the negativity CCBs create. But here's my understanding of why I think they still get elected to top positions:

- Their superior intellect aids them in the process. They deliver what is important for the bosses, stakeholders, and the organisation. Even when the employees are going through a crisis at the office, CCBs ensure that the deadline and goals are met. As long as they achieve results, they do not want to upset the balance by asking too many questions.

- CCBs are very good at upward management. They know how to approach a certain client or even the stakeholders and how to convince them. In a nutshell, they are experts in manipulating and moulding people. They are very well acquainted with the game, and they understand the give-and-take ratio; that is to say, how much and what they have to give in order to get what they want. They are adept at maintaining appearances.

- They practice the 'flog and the slog' mantra, which dictates that they flog people very hard, which will compel them to slog harder. At the end of the day, tangible results will be visible.

- They control the power of information. They disrupt the natural flow of information from the lower level to the higher level. They filter the news or the information that is ideally supposed to flow from one point to another. They are brilliant at keeping the headaches away from the bosses. Whenever something comes up, they say things like, "Don't worry, I will take care of it. You go to the golf course, take the rest of the day off," or "Oh, that? Don't waste your time on that. I am here for those kinds of things." This naturally puts the super boss at ease because, like everybody else, all they really want to do is to delegate and move on. And this makes a CCB a perfect candidate.

- Stakeholders also prefer these talented but aggressive people because it is they who really get the job done, whatever tactics they use – be it their hysteria power, their pester power, or even their nagging power.

Is it bad to be a taskmaster? Not at all. But like I said in the earlier chapter, intent is everything. Are they doing it for the growth of the organisation, or are they doing it for their own selfish goals? Do they care about how it impacts the culture or the attrition rate? By now, we know that CCBs can have a spiralling effect on the productivity of a team or an organisation, with their repetitive attacks or pressure.

However, their innate adeptness helps them get away with it. They either blame others or cover up their mistakes so well that it saves them from any possible conflict that might incriminate them.

When There is a Shift of Gears:

- What happens if the victim shifts from a position of being relational to transactional?

- How does the CCB feel about negotiation or the penalty clause?

- How do they react when you suddenly or slowly change your way of interaction with them – from being virtuous to being practical?

One of the top answers that I have consistently heard from them is, "Oh, the guy has matured." They think that it had to happen, that the guy was foolish, and this is what coming-of-age looks like. With a slight smile, they might also convey an ounce of respect. While there is still a slim chance of CCBs respecting a junior or colleague who stands up to them, the two things they have utter disrespect for are:

- Lack of intellect.

- Lack of competence.

They believe that a person deserves what they get if they lack the competence or the intellect. Like the Colombians, they believe that these people deserve to be taken for a ride, and it is their fault because those are the rules of the game. Don't get me wrong here. I love Colombian culture, people, and stories.

Colombians have a good heart and attitude for life. (I am just referring to the pineapple as an example). But as soon as you try pushing back, like drawing boundaries, negotiating, putting up an empty clause, calling a spade a spade, responding to negativity with negativity, or standing your ground on fairness and justice, they will test you. They will pick a fight with you. They will attempt to make your life miserable in every way.

See, the CCBs had become comfortable abusing you, taking you for a ride, but now, when you are standing up for your right, they are unable to handle it. I would also like to clarify something at this point. This is not just about assertiveness; this is about you gaining clarity at an ontological[22] level.

This is about you changing. This is you being able to see through things. Now, it's not about learning to say no – you might not always say no; sometimes you may say yes, or sometimes you may even keep quiet. This is not about you protecting others from abuse or defending your own rights. It is about bringing a behavioural change to create a conducive and encouraging environment for you.

There are No CCBs

Now, this may not be surprising, but CCBs reject themselves as a possible contender of the category. This process is called 'Otherisation'. Otherisation refers to making a person or group of people seem different, or to consider themselves to be different. It is actually quite a common phenomenon.

Let me give the example of the pandemic. The doctors and the government have, since the beginning, been urging the public to maintain social distancing guidelines. Some do, and some don't. The ones who

---

[22] Ontology: relating to the branch of metaphysics dealing with the nature of being.

'Ontological arguments'

don't follow a mindset somewhat similar to the CCB: "It has happened to them, it can never happen to me." Add to this the concept of otherisation, and other factors come into play, such as privilege, denial, and feelings of superiority. Still, all quite a mess, isn't it?

CCBs think they can outsmart or out-scream everybody else. They know that the common definition of a CCB is unfavourable, and that is why they try to steer clear of being involved or included in the category. I have also asked CCBs if they sleep with a wicked smile. They have responded quite confidently, "I don't know about myself, but I know of certain other CCBs who do."

Again, othering.

Different Types of CCBs

As I mentioned earlier, CCBs can be everywhere. They can be your friend, your parents, your boss, your neighbour, or your teacher. Now, you probably wonder why I keep bringing up parents and may even be aghast at my incriminations against some of them. Let me clarify again, I am not against parents.

But I do know of an extremely attractive lady who constantly mocks her unattractive daughter and blames her for getting her father's genes, which had inadvertently created an inferiority complex in the poor girl. Another CCB parent is a master at making their children feel guilty if they engage in some entertaining or joyful activity when the parents are unwell.

Mankind is truly complex. They can be classified according to varied mental and psychological textures of Sattva[23], Rajas[24], and Tamas[25]. This means there can be different textures of well-intentioned and ill-intentioned people; different textures of evolutionary and devolutionary people; the extent of their ego; the inextricable nature of attachment; the multifariousness of their desire, and the values they put their belief in. Based on the variegation of these traits, will emerge an oppressor or the oppressed.

To understand the different types of CCBs, we have to understand what defines them.

Style Of Communication:

Some of them could be extremely sweet, yet extremely damaging. They could be dishonest and devious under the garb of kindness. On the other hand, some will attack you as soon as they come across you, only to assert their dominance, to drill it into your head that they are the real boss here. While some may wait for a longer period of time to get to know you better, to get under your skin, so they can attack you accordingly.

---

[23] One of the three Gunas (tendencies, qualities, attributes) in Hindu philosophy, Sattva represents things that are pure, divine, and spiritual.

[24] Rajas are innate tendencies or qualities that drive motion, energy and activity. Rajas is sometimes translated as passion, where it is used in the sense of activity, without any particular value and it can contextually be either good or bad.

[25] Tamas means darkness in Sanskrit and is one of the three Gunas.

Intelligence:

Most calcium channel blockers (CCBs) are known for their superior intellect. However, as we know, not all of them are sharp or intellectual. Instead, they are vicious and aggressive. So, their viciousness, selfishness, aggression, and courage – that is to say, their ability to act outwards instead of acting inward – make up for their lack of intellect.

Emotional Abuse:

Some CCBs attack your pride to feed their own ego. Thus, their pride is fulfilled, while yours is damaged. They could be doing it for money, they could be doing it for any material benefit, or they could be doing it to take advantage of your network.

All of us have several layers wrapped around us: matter, body, emotions, intellect, values, and spirituality. Thus, it is very important to be aware of our surroundings. What do I mean by this? Relationships are based on a give-and-take equation and can only be peaceful if the transaction is equal. An equal transaction involves equality at any or all layers put together.

CCBs tend to take, take, and take. They offer nothing apart from relief in their attacks if you comply with their needs. Thus, it is necessary to be aware of the people we surround ourselves with and understand which people draw what energy from us.

Understanding the different kinds of CCBs helps us maintain our sanity and provides us with a clear strategy to deal with the creeps, crooks, or bullies, and correct the give-and-take ratios with the CCBs in our ecosystem.

There is No Word Such As Fear in the CCB Lexicon

Fear. Is that a word you would associate with CCBs? CCBs fear others, probably not. CCBs incite fear, most definitely. But CCBs do have fears. Hard to believe, isn't it?

- They always seem to be aggressive.

- They always have things their own way.

- They scheme their way into putting people on the back foot so that they can get the spotlight.

- They want more than the fair share and justify it by believing it's the right thing.

We have always identified CCBs as the ones who get what they want by hook or by crook. But have we ever paused to wonder what led to them becoming like this? Do they act out of anxiety, or do they just want to fill a vacuum inside?

Every CCB Tends To Follow This Simple Set Of Set Of Rules:

- If you have it, flaunt it.

- If you have the intellect, use it.

- If you can afford to break the rules, do it.

- If you are blessed with the absence of weakness, approval-seeking, or the need to be liked, rejoice.

CCBs have a complete disregard for what society thinks about them as long as their needs are fulfilled. They have an incessant inclination towards attacking a person. Once they do attack, they also have to prove that they are not at fault and that the opposite party instigated it. In some cases, they admit that they were the ones who attacked, but only to add that it was in defence. If they hadn't attacked first, then the opposite party would have.

They have to clear themselves of all blame and affirm that they are superior to the rest in every possible aspect. CCBs operate from a place of insecurity, which can be traced back to incidents that have happened earlier in their life, and that is their fear.

I once asked a CCB if they would consider themselves a happy person. They don't. They are not emotionally comfortable with people. They often lack a deep connection with people, with whom they can nonchalantly share their miseries. They are always in attack mode since it is embedded in their system. Their domineering attitude of always wanting the upper hand upsets the balance in their relationships, whatever they might be.

They miss the simple pleasures such as bonding with close ones and active, happy participation in their ecosystem. Because of their predatory nature, people hesitate to share their inner lives with them. Even if they are with somebody, they can never entirely let their walls down. They will never be able to expose their true or softer side.

How CCBs Wield Their Power

As human beings, we operate at many levels—material, physical, emotional, intellectual, and spiritual. This is somewhat like the five koshas or sheaths propagated by yoga; it is believed that we are all made up of five bodies, and each one is encased within the other—quite like the Russian Matryoshka dolls. To attain total happiness and well-being, it is important to take care of all the koshas.

Now, let's draw a parallel with this to understand how CCBs leverage power.

Material Power:

We know that money rules the world. It has the power to turn wrong into right, to convict the innocent, to further oppress the already oppressed. The one with the most money has the most power. Let me ask you a personal question: who controls the finances in your house? Is it you, a parent, in-law, or spouse?

We all know what material means. In most cases, it translates to something that has a monetary significance or that is of great value. Examples of material power can be a boss holding on to a promotion or not providing you with the resources to proceed with a project. It could also be parents not giving money to their children, even if they can afford it.

To elaborate a little, there are many parents who use money as bait, promising their children that it will all be theirs. The children bite the bait and continue to serve their parents in the hope of this eventuality. Here, money is the material power, and the parent, to an extent, is a CCB. I have seen so many examples where the father controls the money so tightly that it compels the rest of the family to adhere to a lifestyle prescribed by him, and no one has a say in the matter.

Similarly, a CCB boss may exert material power through stringent budget controls. They will link promotion to performance but not release the money for the resources which will aid the performance. Again, I'd like to clarify, I am not insinuating that people who are money-wise or misers are CCBs. I am talking about CCBs who traumatise DGPs by brandishing their control on money.

Physical Power:

Imagine this scenario: you're waiting for the red light to change, and suddenly, a car behind rams into your car. You get down to fight and see that the other car driver is taller and bigger than you and walks menacingly towards you. Would you get aggressive and ask him to pay for the damage, or would you mumble a few curses under your breath and drive away?

This is physical power at play. When a CCB is physically stronger than a DGP, he will use it to his advantage. They manipulate you, play games with you, and take things from you unfairly.

I'll give another example of how appearance can influence behaviour—of both self and of the other person. If we are arguing with a person who is stronger, taller, or bigger than us, or if they have a booming voice, it is intimidating. A CCB with these qualities will take advantage of it to unnerve a DGP.

- It could be a neighbour who takes away your parking spot unfairly and, when confronted, blames you for not utilising it properly; maybe he even threatens you.

- It could also be the policeman who is corrupt. We all know that the police have been granted a certain amount of power to ensure law and order. In any case, we have already established that power corrupts. Thus, there will be some who try to use it unfairly by accepting bribes or giving preferential treatment to the influential ones. If a policeman is a CCB, then he will exert his power or his dominance to prove to you that he is in a superior position and that he can do anything to you. In short, he will do it because he can. I'd like to clarify this is just an example; I have utmost regard for the police force who, despite the dire circumstances they have to work under, continue to toil relentlessly to maintain law and order.

Emotional Power:

In my opinion, emotional power is the most abusive form of power and occurs in our personal and professional lives. For example, when a CCB sees that their spouse is extremely attached to them, they use that to their advantage to get their way. A pampered child who has been refused what he wants will manipulate his/her parents' emotions by throwing a tantrum or using some other drastic measure to get what they want or to solicit sympathy.

A potential CCB in the making. In both cases, they are using manipulation. They know what your weak point is. They will know exactly where to attack you to get their work done or to keep a leash on you.

Needless to say, manipulation is widely prevalent in our professional life too. Suppose you are a sensitive person and one of your CCB colleagues or bosses is aware of that, they might do something intentionally to hurt you. Why? It could be because you cannot stand up to them, or maybe they get sadistic pleasure from seeing someone suffer.

Their aim is to hurt you and humiliate you. In order to achieve what they want, there is nothing that they wouldn't try. Once a CCB decides what they want, they do not listen to their conscience. In fact, if I frame it more crassly, they do not have much of a conscience left anymore.

CCBs can also be great influencers. They can be charming enough to persuade people to do something they don't want to do. Therefore, if you are a part of their group and show resistance and reluctance, they will either throw you out of the group or ignore you, and exclude you from its activities, and make sure that the other members do the same.

For example, CCBs could plan a party and not invite you. CCBs could plan an attack remotely as well. Suppose you are an influencer with a large following, they would troll you. They would leave nasty comments on your posts, or spread lies about you, fabricate evidence, twist your words, and ensure that your credibility is affected.

CCBs have another favourite tactic, and that is not just to hurt or demoralise the DGP, but even to rebuke their hurt by labelling them as martyrs or sympathy-seekers. I call this *Jale par namak chhidakana* (adding salt to the wound, which is a metaphor for adding insult to injury).

They do so even if the DGP has not vocalised their disillusionment; the idea is to find fault in any complaint made by the DGP. Complaining by DGPs is branded as victimhood, not being man enough, or being a sissy!

Intellectual Power:

This is employed when CCBs essentially assert their superiority by leveraging their intellect or knowledge. A brilliant example could be a boardroom meeting. The CCB could be the presenter, or they could be part of the audience, but the intention remains the same – to make the other person appear less intelligent, feel, or look dumb.

If the boss or someone in a superior rank is presenting, they will pick the least informed person from the audience and throw a question at them. For example, let's presuppose that your job is in the creative department and you are not as conversant with technical jargon. They throw technical jargon at you and ask you the question.

Their aim is to humiliate you, and when you will not be able to answer the question in a room full of people, their motive will be fulfilled. The same holds true for the reverse. If the CCB is somebody from the audience, they will throw a question at you on an issue or topic they know you are not conversant with. This would make them appear more intelligent than you. Not only do they derive pleasure from this, but the other person's humiliation feeds their ego.

Another example could be seen when dealing with professionals such as a doctor or a lawyer. You will always find doctors or lawyers using terminology that the common man is not familiar with, and sometimes they are reluctant to elaborate on the same.

Again, don't get me wrong. I am not trying to imply that all doctors or lawyers are CCBs. I am simply using their reference to illustrate this point.

Spiritual Power:

We can borrow the classic example of the misuse of spiritual power from so-called spiritual gurus. There are many sincere ones who have adopted the divine path to help people deal with their problems, but we are referring to the ones who are here to help themselves. They use your vulnerability to extort money from you in the guise of conducting pujas (prayer ceremony) and donating to their charities. Should you refuse, they will manipulate you into thinking that you are defying your spiritual path, and this will lead to your doom.

The purpose of this book is to bring to the fore the selfish and manipulative nature of the CCBs. DGPs may not find it easy to combat them, but let me assure you, it is not impossible either, and this book is designed to help them do so. If you are a DGP, study and familiarise yourself with the various weapons that the CCB pulls out of his armoury, then pull out your bulletproof vest.

Once you understand their techniques, your misplaced virtuosity[26], gullibility, and pseudo-morality will dissipate. You will sharpen up by becoming true to yourself and choosing your battle strategies wisely. Start standing up to them slowly, take baby steps; you will experience certain emotions which may seem alien but, slowly, you will get accustomed to.

Start becoming aware of what is happening in your head and your heart. You may choose to semi-stand up for yourself, then withdraw, then stand up, then withdraw, then stand up, then celebrate; everyone has a different journey. You will be scared of failing, but that is natural. It will take time, but you would be moving to a life of greater happiness and authenticity. Once you rise above the fear, once you stop getting traumatised, you will be able to live your life to its potential.

Silence is Another Manipulation Technique Used by CCBs

We know CCBs use their personality or their position to exert power over weaker mortals. We also know that

---

[26] Misplaced virtuosity is trying to be virtuous in the wrong place and is covered in Chapter 1.

they leverage their physical attributes to intimidate others. In your mind, you are seeing a tall, gregarious, loud-mouthed (and probably foul-mouthed) CCB talking his way through. What if I told you that sometimes, a CCB's often-used manipulation technique is silence!

Sometimes, in a conversation, you may find a DGP blabbering incessantly while the CCB listens quietly. The DGP feels compelled to reveal their thoughts, their experiences, and what they have done throughout the day. Why is that? One reason could be their discomfort with silence—most people are. Silence can be unpleasant.

People typically feel the pressure to break the silence with any conversation as it makes them squirm physically and mentally; they have a hundred (mostly negative) thoughts running through their head. CCBs leverage this discomfort to their advantage and prod for information with questions like, 'How come you have become so boring these days? You don't even share anything with me anymore.

This could accentuate the DGP's insecurity, and the fear of abandonment could lead them to reveal more than is required. They will, therefore, do anything to prove they are good people and avoid any conflict situation.

I'm sure all of you are familiar with the Pavlov[27] experiment with dogs, which led to the theory of conditioning. In this case, the CCB is Pavlov, and the

---

[27] "Pavlov" most commonly refers to the Russian physiologist Ivan Pavlov, known for his experiments on classical conditioning. His work demonstrated how animals can learn to associate stimuli, leading to a conditioned response.

DGP is the dog. The CCB's interrogative nature is like the bell—it prompts the DGP to talk. Bear in mind, DGPs have an uncomfortable relationship with silence. It creates feelings of guilt that they are not honouring their friendship by sharing personal details or that they are not doing their job well. This makes them extremely talkative even when they do not want to talk, as it helps them to divert themselves from this bizarre discomfort.

This marks the birth of the people-pleasing attitude. We are often very quick to dismiss this behaviour as 'attention-seeking' or 'spineless'. We label DGPs with derogatory terms and look down upon them, but have you ever considered what makes them so subservient? As you can see, the people-pleasing attitude is a trauma response. It is an unavoidable voice within them that forces them to behave in a way that will make people like them.

The approval they get in response to their pleasing behaviour becomes a major source of happiness. They cannot make people mad at them or disagree with them because all these actions will ultimately lead to them being disliked, and that is something they cannot live with.

DGPs must react with shrewdness and smartness. If you find a CCB going quiet again and provoking you for not talking enough, you can firmly respond with, "I have shared what I had to share. What's up with you?"

At this point, they might get defensive and say, "Why are you turning the gun on me? I am asking you a question. Why don't you answer?"

You have to be very careful about not giving away your fears by being aggressive or nervous; tone of voice is an indicator of emotional state. Be calm and confident when you respond to that statement with something along the lines of, "Yeah, I know. I have shared what was there to say. Now, you tell me what's up. Looks like you are trying to avoid something here."

To be very honest, and you may hate me for this, the only way you can get through to a CCB is by behaving like them because that is the only language they understand. You have to study their behaviour, adopt their manipulative strategy, and use it against them.

To help you understand the circumstances a little better, let me give you an example. You have a presentation with the board. You are done with it, save for a few finishing touches. Your colleague asks you what you are doing. You share your idea with him as you see it as a practice run.

He commends you and wishes you luck, which really boosts your confidence. The next day, at the meeting, you realise that he is set to present before you. When he does, you see your idea on the screen. He takes full credit for it as the original creator.

If something like this has happened to you before, then you probably have a very good idea of what these people are like. The first step to avoid the blatant plagiarising of your idea would be to avoid sharing any information with these people. Well, whether you would like to avoid them for the rest of your life is absolutely up to you.

If they continue to pester you about it, firmly reply, "Oh, I am honoured that you are interested in my idea. Your presence at the presentation would really be encouraging." Turn the situation around with a response that is polite and massages his ego.

This is what we say, *sap mare lathi na tute* (killing the snake without breaking the stick), which is a reference for getting your work done without losing anything. In this case, the snake is the CCB, and the stick is your relationship, which you do not want to break.

CHAPTER 6

WHAT MAKES CCBS WHO THEY ARE

6.1 Role of Child Psychology

Let us begin with a flashback, by going way back to the day we were born. Every child's progress—be it emotionally or physically—is measured in four different stages.

- Infant: 0-12 months.

- Toddler: 1-3 years.

- Preschool: 3-5 years.

- School: 5-18 years.

Most children complete their schooling by 18 years, and what comes after is the young adult period, which is considered to be from 18 years to 22 years. At this time, most young adults go away to college or look for a job (either in or away from their city) and try to build a support system from the ground up.

All in all, they try to acclimatise themselves to a drastically different environment. Most heartbreaks occur during this period. This is the time where they become aware of social issues, become aware of themselves emotionally, intellectually, or sexually. They try to explore themselves and new activities.

In any case, let's go back to what we were talking about in the beginning; about the infant to the preschool period, which is considered to be the most important time in shaping the personality of a child.

"Who am I?" Baby steps to maturity

Through these stages, every child finds themselves and forms a personality.

"Am I Safe?" Infancy

Safety, security. How important are these things to us?

Immensely.

I'll give you a very simple example. Imagine you have relocated to a new city and have been looking for a flat or a commercial premise for your business. After you have evaluated the advantages of the location, and maybe even before you conclude at the price, what is the first question you ask your broker, the question that constantly plagues your mind? "Is it safe for me to be here?"

From a very young age, we learn to differentiate between what is good for us and what is bad for us, or what is considered to be dangerous and what is considered to be safe. This is the age where we realise this. Of course, there is no denying that parents have an extremely important role to play here, but they are not the only ones who act as guardians.

The society we live in, the teachers who guide us, the friends we make, all the different people we come across, and the different people we associate ourselves with—each of them has an extremely important part to play in the way our personalities are shaped or in the way our ideologies are formed.

The first brick that lays the foundation of our personality is our understanding of safety. According to our understanding, our strategies are segmented into *Dukh Nivritti* or *Sukh Prapti*[28]. If we sense that we are in an unsafe space, our strategies will be directed towards protecting ourselves from anything dangerous.

Similarly, if we are convinced that we are in a safe space, we will explore ourselves, open ourselves, and initiate a search for happiness. When in a safe space, our primary thought process or instincts do not focus on protecting ourselves. Therefore, we are not pressured; we are not stressed.

We can think about ourselves, and what do we try to do for ourselves? We try to make ourselves happy. Similarly, when a child is in a safe space, the child is more prone to being a happy adult.

Now that we have understood the importance of being in a safe space, let us go through the factors that determine our need and search for safety or security for ourselves.

- Touch

- Feel

---

[28] According to the Vedanta, we pursue things that are 'sukh prapti', i.e. pleasant or joyful in nature and avoid 'dukh nivritti', i.e. painful or unpleasant situations.

- Sound

"What do I want?" Toddler

This is the second stage where children realise that they are a separate entity from their mother. Therefore, they understand that they have their separate needs, wants, or desires. This stage enables our ability to choose or our capacity to decide for ourselves what we want. Since we are born, we cannot understand that we are a different entity. If you look at it, what are we? Who are we? We are just a pound of flesh that grew inside a woman's abdomen, and then we were born. Thus, physically, we are a pound of flesh cut from our mother's body.

Now, we do not have the intellect to fully fathom what is going on, but what we can make out is that we are what our mothers are. Since the very beginning, we spend most of our time in their laps, being breastfed, or being lulled to sleep. Thus, when we open our eyes, we see our mother. The last thing we see before we close our eyes is also our mother. I know there are a lot of people who would argue that many mothers, especially working ones or those who live in huge joint families, may not have the time to be with their children at all times. That is true.

A child develops the strongest attachment with the person they spend the most time with. However, having said that, nothing can surpass the bond a mother has with their child. Even if the mother is busy during the day and the only time she spends with her children is in the morning or at night, children will always recognise their mother.

Therefore, every child goes through a period where they consider themselves to be a part of their mother, and it is only at this stage of realisation that they understand they are a separate entity. This is also when a child grows their ability to express what they truly desire.

"What is My Sexuality?" Preschool

At this age, a child becomes aware of their sexuality, i.e. whether they are a girl, boy, or transgender. I know I am listing down only three of them, while many more genders have come to be in this era. Just to be clear, I am not denouncing their existence.

What I'm trying to say is that at this age, a child cannot understand if their existence or identity is placed outside the three genders or sexes that are already presented to them. That realisation, which is equally important, comes at a later part in their life, that is to say, when they turn into a young adult.

Apart from their sexual awareness, they also comprehend feelings. They learn what feelings are, how it affects them, and how to process it. The processing part is not limited to just the period of preschool; it goes beyond that and sometimes, a child only learns to process feelings when they are in school.

It is also an extremely important age for emotional development. If a child experiences a healthy environment, then they are confident to express their emotions to themselves and others.

"How to Deal with the World?" School

This period is only a continuation of the preschool age where the emotional development of the personality is initiated. In the preschool period, they learn how to express their feelings to themselves, and in this period, they also learn how to communicate their feelings to the world.

This stage is divided into these three binaries:

- Cooperate/Compete
- Synergise/Nynergise
- Friction/Lubrication

Their decision to partake in any one part of the binaries comprises the foundation of their personalities. Research shows that people who go through these four stages positively – i.e. by understanding the concept of safety, expressing their needs, understanding their sexuality, getting in touch with their feelings, and communicating the same to the world – can take part in both cooperation and competition, synergising and nynergising, friction, and lubrication.

These people turn out to be more confident in themselves, with how they look or how their personality has shaped up. These people create a true self for themselves. On the other hand, the people who go through these stages with negativity are repressed under a false self. The source of all psychological problems lies in staying in the false self and burying the true self.

Why do we cocoon ourselves inside a false self?

What happens when your emotional needs are not taken care of in childhood? What are the factors that pollute or wound them at the four stages of your development?

When an infant comes into the world, they come with their uniqueness or their atypical DNA footprint that sets them apart from the rest. We all know that it is impossible for our fingerprints to be replicated. Similarly, we are born with different sets of uniqueness.

However, they can only manifest that if they receive a healthy upbringing from the very beginning. We have already established that the first step for the infant is to recognise a safe or an unsafe space around them.

Let's say that the infant is not welcomed with safe energy. They are not given the vibe, the energy, the hugs, the touches, or the sounds of safety. Their knowledge of an unsafe ecosystem or an unsafe environment could be manifested in extreme anxiety later in life. They will constantly be under attack; they will always be in a defensive mode. Their lives will be filled with 'what if' questions:

- What if I lose all my money?

- What if they find out something about me?

- What if they leave me?

- What if I do this, and it turns into a mess?

- What if I am to blame for this?

- What if there is a bully in the audience?

Their fears may be irrational, but their mind tricks them to believe otherwise. Their whole nervous system is so strung-up and shrivelled that we label it as anxiety, whereas the culprit is the lack of safety and security. At the toddler stage, a child is supposed to become aware of themselves as an individual entity.

This is when they realise that they can ask for things, and if that realisation is stunted or obstructed in any way, what comes as a result is a lifetime of psychological issues. I am not talking about a child being pampered; what I am trying to say is that they must be provided with what they need.

Let me explain this with an example. Suppose a child says that he/she wants to eat a particular thing, wants a toy, or even a pen. They must be given that. However, if they ask for something impossible, which cannot be given, they must not be reprimanded or made to feel that it is not their position to ask, or that they are not allowed to ask for what they want.

If a parent does not want to give a child something, they must not rebuke them for that. They must explain their reasons in a way that a toddler would understand. A parent must never make a child feel like they are authoritative and will decide what they can give the child. This will pollute the child's emotional self, and they will never be comfortable or confident enough to state what they really want, even if it's their basic needs.

For example, let's say everyone is going to a non-vegetarian restaurant. You are not fond of non-vegetarian food and you would like to have vegetarian food. Now, since you have not developed that confidence or ability to speak up for what you want, you will be compelled to go along with what most people want. If you do, you will constantly feel that you are being abandoned, disliked, or not being taken seriously.

If you study the basic need of a child's mind, you will see that all they want is safety, which arrives from true and unconditional love. Now, there must not be any confusion between love and admiration. Admiration or approval is what a child gets in return for an activity they complete or an action they take.

Love is something every child should ideally receive, irrespective of what they do and what they do not do. Love must be unconditional. The problem arises when the child seeks love, but all they receive is admiration. For example, when a child does something a parent wants them to do, they receive admiration. They get positive energy and confuse this admiration with love.

However, at this point, they form a distorted definition of love in their psyche. To them, love becomes transactional. When the child does something that pleases the parent or another person, they fill themselves up with positive energy. It makes them feel comfortable, but it does not offer them safety. They try to become what their parents want them to become to fill the vacuum inside. Thus begins the foundation of approval-seeking behaviour.

Preschool

If a toddler moves up to a preschool without their needs being met, they will carry with themselves an incomplete or stunted emotional growth, which will hamper their personality. At this stage, they will want to be in touch with their feelings and express them. If the parents shame them for asking for their needs or wants to be fulfilled, they will stop asking. They will no longer be confident enough to express their feelings or desires. So, what do they do?

They cocoon themselves inside a false self. They either state false feelings, or they stop expressing themselves. Instead, they attune themselves to the expectations of others in search of the admiration they mistook for love. These people are extremely sympathetic and empathetic towards others.

In the last stage, when the child is in school, they are supposed to deal with the world and express their feelings to them. Now, if their overall growth has been obstructed and incomplete, it culminates in this stage as an inability to work properly.

What Issues Surface The Most?

- If they are to work in a team, not only will they be an unfit leader, but they will also be unable to cooperate with others.

- They will never be able to unleash their true potential. That is to say, despite having the capabilities, they will face problems at implementing or expressing them. As a result, they will never be good enough.

- They will never be able to foster a healthy relationship of interdependence with people. They will never be able to entirely trust a person or call their bluff because they cannot trust themselves at all.

Acting In/Acting Out

I am sure you are dying to ask the question: how does a CCB or a DGP become who they are?

Their personality navigates this direction for them, and this can be traced to nature or nurture. For instance, if they are born intelligent, they realise that they can use their intelligence in several ways. This is where the famous adage 'power corrupts' is at play.

Their intelligence becomes their weapon, their 'kavach' (a safety shield). It gives them nerves of steel and the courage to push boundaries, to play with people's minds and emotions, and as a result, they play havoc with people's lives. These kinds of CCBs are categorised as Quad D-Intelligent and Ill-intentioned, the Shakuni bosses. They are intelligent and exploit the weaknesses or vulnerabilities of DGPs unabashedly and deliberately.

Why does it come to that? If your emotional self has not been taken care of in your infancy or toddler stage, you start to live in a false self. At this point, you either act out, or you begin to act in. Let me explain what I mean by these terms. Acting out refers to an attitude, a state of being that is sadistic and insolent.

The person is determined to take revenge from another person and torture them until they are satisfied or get what they want. On the other hand, 'acting in' is the opposite— the person blames him or herself for every bad thing that happens.

Let's take a person whose emotional self is not entirely developed; they do not feel safe enough to express their needs. If they act out, they assume an aggressive stance with their intelligence. The thought that dictates their behaviour is—since I have not received safety in my childhood, I will get it for myself by ruling over you.

Such a person considers their ruthlessness as the safety that will fill their vacuum, but the sad part is that even if they continue with this attitude all through their life, they will still never feel psychologically safe. They mistake control for safety. They try to gain control over as many things as they can. They make sure that the people around them or the environment around them are defined by what they want, and then they mislabel this control with safety.

Let's look at this categorically. Suppose you were not cared for in your infant stage, your needs, wants, and desires were left unfulfilled, and thus, your emotional personality remained incomplete. Your mind could never anchor itself to the things or even the assurance you craved, even when you asked for it.

So, at this point, the CCB acts out and says, "I will get what I do not have from you." Having this constant need or want from you is a behaviour we call 'acting out'.

If a person faces obstructions or hindrances at the preschool level, they feel suppressed, which hampers their ability to get in touch with their feelings and, inevitably, to express them. They expect you, the DGP, to fulfil these unmet demands. They will bully you into allowing them to dominate you to get all the attention. If they were not showered with love and care as a child, they invent various ways by which they can extract that from other people.

Now, let's discuss what categorises 'acting in'. As the name suggests, if their emotional development is stunted or obstructed, some people don't look out for help, they look within. In fact, they do not look for help at all. They hold themselves responsible for everything and constantly focus on their flaws.

At the same time, they crave all the love and attention that they have never received as a child. True to their nature, they consider themselves at fault for not being loved. As a result, they develop people-pleasing behaviour to gain a sense of safety, as they feel that these people will not abandon them.

'Acting in' and 'acting out' are different ways of seeking safety, love, care, or admiration and are the primary processes adopted by CCBs and DGPs to address their emotional void. No one can argue that the strategies employed by a CCB (acting out) are superior to those of a DGP (acting in), or vice versa.

6.2 Parents—The Primary Players

Why do parents fail to provide the child with what they need? Could it be because they do not love the child, or because they love themselves more? Do they do it deliberately, or are they unaware of what is happening?

What I am going to say is going to shock you. Unless a parent is very advanced, mature, or experienced, they qualify as 'adult children'. They might have a vacuum as their needs might have gone unfulfilled when they were children. These are the needs they might have had for the past 20 or so years, probably needs that went unmet since the time they were an infant.

Therefore, even at this age, they are constantly in search of safety. They, therefore, try to get that safety from their own little child. They know that this little child cannot pack their bags and leave; he or she is, after all, a toddler, a pre-schooler, or an infant. So, they fulfil their need for safety from that child, knowing fully well that these children will do anything they say.

The child will listen to the parent, and if, in any case, the parent does not comply with them, they will not be able to scold the parent. Thus, the parent can rule over them at any time. By bossing over the child, a parent feels that they have a permanent companion in the child – that companion, under no circumstances, can leave them.

Therefore, instead of providing safety to the child, they try to seek safety from the child. Now, if the parents have grown up in an unhealthy environment, this means that they too were forbidden from expressing their needs or their wants. What they do to the child is that they start expressing everything that they couldn't have done until now and expect the child to fulfil these.

In some cases, the parents may become so demanding that they go to the length of impressing upon the child that it is their responsibility to keep the parents happy. To add salt to the wound, they create guilt by reinforcing that it was they who brought the child into the world, so this is the least the child can do for them.

Sometimes, parents may ask the child to do something for them, which fuels the child's motivation. When the child completes their assignment, they are rewarded— not with love, but with admiration. Therefore, they understand that to receive that positive stroke, they have to complete or do something in return.

As I mentioned earlier, the child receives a distorted definition of love in their mind, which registers as a transactional relationship. Sometimes, a child may take on certain responsibilities that should actually be the parents' role. Instead of enjoying their own childhood or taking care of their own self, they are expected to be busy taking care of their parents.

What people do not want to understand is that a child is not supposed to mature up so prematurely; they are supposed to enjoy their childhood. They cannot turn into an adult in their childhood. When a child grows up in a healthy environment, they become creative and inventive. They may want to carve a toy out of a vegetable, or they might want to paint the sky pink.

However, if you lump a lot of responsibility onto the child in the hope that you're training your child to become disciplined, you are not allowing the playfulness in them to grow. The child will almost never be in touch with their own feelings. In fact, they will be in touch with the needs of the parents. And if this continues, they could miss out on the boldness or the naturalness that is imperative for them to grow.

An 'adult child' parent expresses their needs to their child to fulfil the emotional vacuum that their own parents created – the care their parents never took, their elders, or the powerful people they were surrounded with who ignored their needs. By doing so, they disable the child's capacity to speak for themselves. The child cannot say what they want; the child cannot state if they're happy, sad, or hungry.

Four kinds of wounded parents

Now, let's summarise the four kinds of wounded parents..

- The first one looks for safety in their child and tries to gain that by bossing them around.

- The second kind of wounded parents try to satisfy their needs through their children. They express admiration to their children when their needs are met.

- The third kind expresses their feelings to the children, instead of letting the children seek a safe space and express their true desires.

- The fourth kind of wounded parents are not very comfortable with the interpersonal aspects of cooperation or competition with the rest of the world. They expect their children to fill in for their job roles.

The child gets so invigorated to receive that positive stroke of 'love' that when they fail, they develop a severe case of anxiety. I know what you are thinking; parents do so much for the children. Instead of expressing gratitude, how dare the child, the outsider, or even the author be questioning the parents' intent? I would like to clarify; I have nothing against parents.

Neither am I instituting that children be ungrateful to their parents. Our scriptures, *shastra*[29], and wise books across all religions preach about how we should always be thankful to our parents. We owe it to our parents. We have taken from them, and we have to repay our debt.

I just want to clarify here that my only intention is to understand the deeper psychologies, or the blueprints, archetypes, and patterns of automatic behaviour or impulses that we develop, and how we come to develop them. A good chunk of this work is based on research by top-notch psychologists who are trying to explain incomprehensible behaviour or habits.

---

[29] Shastra is a Sanskrit word that means "precept, rules, manual, compendium, book or treatise" in a general sense.

Nature vs Nurture: Its Genesis

Many people are of the opinion that nature does this to them. Many others point a finger at nurture. With the help of child psychology, in this section, we will try to understand what goes on in nurture. I would like to once again reiterate that this is not about parents bashing or them externalising the problem.

I am not trying to point fingers at parents and get people to absolve their responsibility. It could also be very wrong to assume that as soon as a person turns into a parent, they are automatically blessed with the power of parenting. It doesn't work like that either. Becoming a biological parent does not qualify one to be a competent guardian.

Every child is different. Therefore, they need to be dealt with differently. In fact, the people who have already been a great parent to one or two children may still find it somewhat difficult to gel with the third child. As I said, not everyone comes with the same blueprint.

Hence, it would be extremely unjustified to blame it entirely on nature or, for that matter, even on nurture. The topic at hand is what happens when the child does not get their basic requirements. Let's delve into that with the help of an analogy.

Imagine you are weak in a particular subject at school. You must feel safe to voice this. If you have to ask questions several times, it is because deep down you feel safe in the knowledge that this will not irritate the class teacher. You may feel that she may lose patience, but it is acceptable and safe to express discomfort and not resort to a false self to pacify the teacher.

Having said that, I must mention that students sometimes find it difficult to address an issue to the teacher, and the reason behind this is not always limited to the fact that the teacher is unapproachable. There have been several circumstances where, despite being assured by the teacher, the student could not muster up the courage to talk about it.

Therefore, the only option left for them is to be attentive from the very beginning. What happens if you do not pay extra attention to the subject? If you neither understand the subject nor alert your teacher about this, you will not attain the skill. If you do not attain the skill, then you are a misfit for the team engagement, and that will put you at a disadvantage when contributing in an interdependent setting.

It will impact your confidence as you will realise that you do not have the character to apply for a relevant internship or a job. Your character is impacted because you are not being authentic to yourself, to your emotions, to the teacher, to the moment, and character development cannot happen without authenticity, without being true to yourself.

Thus, if you do not have the character, then you lose out on an internship. Without an internship, you do not have any experience, which will, in the end, be extremely challenging for you while you try to land a job.

Do you understand what I'm trying to say here? A child has to feel safe first to feel confident enough to ask for what they want and express their thoughts. Eventually, they will only be able to interact with the world if they can express their desires.

6.3 Understanding Emotional Vacuum

What is an emotional vacuum? It is a feeling of emptiness, of being devoid of any emotions, and it is a state that can happen regularly in a person's life. What are the strategies for dealing with this emotional energy? One of the most recommended ways is to cooperate with it, to partner with it.

Consider your emotional energy as your childlike energy and yourself as the adult who is the protector of that childlike energy. It is important for the 'adult you' to accept and protect your emotional childlike energy in order to feel comfortable in your skin. If there is a disconnect between the two, this could lead to an uncomfortable dissonance, which could create an unexplained emotional vacuum.

When these two personalities coexist, they partner and help each other. Try to ask yourself, what is the role of your inner child? Do they want to be inventive, vivacious, and creative, or do they just want to be happy? Inner child is another name for your emotional self and sometimes the unresolved emotional self. The inner child is a form of energy that can either be in a place of sulking and sadness or be channelised into making life wonderful.

This energy is responsible for so much exploration and adventure for the child to engage in. When this kind of energy is shelved, it keeps pushing us from below; it keeps creating trouble for us, making us aware of its existence. When an adult finally gets in touch with the inner child, they unlock energy or a side of them that they haven't seen before.

There are enough psychological experiments that prove that, in this scenario, the adult holds the hand of the child and says, "Come, let's do it together. That way, your spontaneity won't land you in trouble because I am here to guide you."

The child says, "Let's channelise this adult hotness or excessive caution and energise that through my childlike energy."

So, getting in touch with this childlike energy is kind of unlocking the repressed energies. These underdeveloped energies can sometimes explode. That is why it is necessary for the adult self to be present at all times. There are multiple ways in which these energies are stifled, but there is always a way out.

Four steps an adult must take

- **Potency:** You encourage the child to get in touch with their inner emotional energy.

- **Permission:** You give them permission to process the energy.

- **Protection**: You assure the child that you are there and that you will be there for the rest of the journey.

Practice: Finally, encourage them to begin the process.

It is very interesting how, sometimes, the emotional self degenerates into different types of roles. For example, let's imagine that in a particular house, there is an intimacy vacuum between the parents. That is to say, the father and the mother do not share a healthy relationship.

Now, this can adversely affect a child's emotional development. They don't usually understand what is happening because their emotional or intellectual self is not entirely developed. However, a tendency that has been largely witnessed in children is that they assume the responsibility of this unhealthy relationship between their parents.

They feel they have to do something about it. So they start doing 'mature things' to please their parents in the hope that this will put their parents in a better mood, which, in turn, makes them feel safe. This act of trying to be mature creates a false self; if the child were to express their true self, they would've cried or thrown a tantrum and questioned their parents on why he or she wasn't being cared for.

Instead, the child slips into adult behaviour, which is contradictory to their core, and in the process loses touch with their true self and emotions. What children need for the development of their emotional selves is unconditional love, but what they get instead is admiration in terms of negotiated reality.

What do children do now?

One of the first things they do is try to become surrogate parents. They end up taking care of their younger sibling. They try to become the surrogate husband by giving their mother a shoulder to cry on. They take up too much responsibility and behave like an adult. As a result, they miss out on their own childhood. They miss the chance to manifest their energies, to feel the emotions, or the ability to get in touch with it through their psychic fingerprint.

Another role the child may assume is to become the scapegoat. They hold themselves responsible for everything bad that happens. They look at themselves as a pitiable creature who is only capable of causing unhappiness for everyone. They start believing that their poor marks in class are the cause of their parents' lack of happiness. Even when the CCB comes in and bullies them or tortures them, they blame themselves for that.

In another scenario, the child becomes an achiever. When they don't receive any love or attention, they channelise all their energy into one particular thing and excel themselves at it. Now, you might say that it is a good thing that they have channelised all their tension into one thing and achieved something in life. Yes, maybe, but at what cost? They created a false self for themselves, which stunted their emotional development. Now, they are no longer looked at as a child; they are looked at as the one who is going to bail them out. They are looked at as the *family ki shaan* (pride of the family).

The Development of Emotional Personality and Its Importance

There are many factors that contribute to the development of our personality, including physical attributes such as height, weight, body structure, and looks, as well as intellectual abilities which involve our beliefs, feelings, behaviour, and attitude that we draw upon when confronted with various situations.

And emotional intelligence that allows us to remain calm, stable, and balanced in the face of adversity. While all the three attributes grow through the various stages of life, it is the emotional attribute that sets the foundation for our future growth and healthy personality development.

It is necessary for the emotional self to develop during the various stages of growing up. What I mean is, our emotions develop positively when we feel safe and secure, when our wants are acknowledged and fulfilled, and when we are allowed to express what we truly feel rather than what we are expected to feel, i.e. being authentic to yourself. This empowers us with confidence and is what will empower us to handle CCBs.

Our feelings, our emotions are the only things we have that truly belong to us. Therefore, it is important to recognise and accept them. There is no right or wrong in how you feel. Take as much time as you need, but be completely honest with yourself; do not portray what is expected of you, as this will create inner conflict, which will further your position in the battle against CCBs.

If you have grown up under the umbrella of safety, you will not fear your feelings. You understand that you have needs and that there is no shame or guilt in expressing them. You need to be able to express your feelings and engage with the world in an authentic, meaningful, and enjoyable way.

To understand whether you are capable of dealing with a CCB, you must go back to your infancy. People can express themselves honestly and authentically only if they have experienced an environment of safety in the infant stage. And if, for any reason, you have not experienced that, you have to drill it in you that CCBs can affect you psychologically only if you give them the power to do so.

Repeat after me, "I will protect my inner child and help it feel safe so that I do not feel the need for the CCB's supply of approval-seeking behaviour. My conviction in myself will be my oxygen and give me the strength and safety to resist and confront the CCB."

You must reinforce the truth that it is acceptable to express or fulfil your needs when confronting the CCB, and neither is that selfish nor does it make you a bad person. After all, they ruthlessly fulfil their own needs under the garb of self-care, so it is wrong of them to label you as selfish when it comes to fulfilling yours.

When a DGP is being confronted, certain emotions will overwhelm you, making you feel uncomfortable. Even if it is a losing battle, accept your feelings without being aggressive or defensive and express them without sugar-coating them.

I must warn you, though, the outcome may be far from pleasant, but you will have the satisfaction of being true to yourself and not be torn between expressing what you want and living an imaginary life according to somebody else's expectations. Likewise, when the DGP is interacting with a CCB, the DGP should draw boundaries and set rules of engagement that are fair and enriching for all the team members.

It is important to develop one's emotional self and live your truth rather than live with the false self that has been outlined by the CCB. A DGP is a person who typically survives on the oxygen supply of approval-seeking behaviour; they mistake admiration for love and are willing to do anything to get that oxygen from the CCB. The CCB realises this and preys on this.

Now, for the critical part; when the DGP tries to break free from the tyrannical, manipulative behaviour of the CCB by attending workshops on assertiveness and courageous conversations, he is faced with unexplained psychological blockages. His energy does not flow. He tries to be courageous but gets tears in his eyes or explodes.

He tries to draw boundaries, but is once again drawn into the web of deceit. He then declares that he has been like this from the very onset of his childhood. He does not realise that all this has been hard-wired into his brain and has formed synaptic connections because of his growing-up years.

He does not understand that unless his emotional self matures through the four phases, he will not feel psychologically or emotionally comfortable to deal with his own 'silence/violence' emotions or vibrations. He reads pop psychology, turns to meditation, and self-help gurus (teacher) but finds no recourse; the undeveloped inner child continues to seek safety and fills up the emotional vacuum with the wrong people and the wrong chances.

This is why we link child psychology to the handling of CCBs. We need to understand that unless we learn to make our emotional inner child feel safe, we may respond to the tactics of the CCBs with extreme, rather than balanced behaviour.

I want YOU, the reader, to understand that if we do not tackle the raw, primal, unexplained energy running through our nerves and the hormones that immobilise us when we are in the presence of CCBs, we may be digging at the wrong place to strike psychological gold. Hence, it is essential to sort out these deep-rooted emotional matters by following the Quad 4 model(s).

CHAPTER 7

TIME TO TAKE A STAND-HANDLING CCBS

Up to now, we have focused our discussion on the characteristics of a DGP and a CCB. What we have successfully established is that, in most cases, a DGP is a puppet at the mercy or the whims of a CCB.

In this chapter, we will focus on what a DGP can do to get out of this vicious cycle and take a stand for themselves.

7.1 Preparing for Battle

Who does the DGP turn to to seek refuge from this kind of brutality?

When our mental health takes a toll, we seek professional help from a psychologist or a psychiatrist. The therapy, medication, and support they provide help us untangle our thoughts and truly understand the chaos within. Unfortunately, in the Indian context, and especially in some societies, seeking professional help is still frowned upon, and this misconception can pose a barrier.

In any case, my primary intention is not to talk about mental health. We have now confirmed that the DGP needs some support—be it physiological, emotional, ontological, or interpersonal. Keep in mind, these people have learnt about pseudo-virtuosity and they tend to be more gullible than non-DGPs. Hence, their reactions are mindless and more transparent.

What are they supposed to do when they are tormented by their near and dear ones in professional and personal relationships alike? They can receive help from their friends, parents, or a like-minded community. Sometimes, talking to a stranger also does the trick because it is easier to share your trauma or your untold secrets with a person that you have never been introduced to before.

In some cases, these strangers are licensed psychologists or psychiatrists, and this is a good option as the feedback, solution, and support are unbiased and unemotional.

Another place most people turn to is social or spiritual clubs. One of the most interesting things that attract people to these clubs is their nonchalance about one's caste, class, religion, race, or even sex. This allows a person to get to know one another without being classified into different boxes, and the connection is only defined by shared interests or defining characteristics.

The support these friendships provide further helps a DGP to conquer their fear of a CCB. However, these people need to have certain qualities to be able to help you. What are these qualities now?

- **Empathy**

Empathy is one of the most important qualities for a person to have when they are your first choice for help.

How will they understand what you are going through if they do not empathise with you?

Notice how I have used the word 'empathy' and not 'sympathy'; the latter does not require them to understand you by coming up or down to your level. When a person empathises with you, they try to feel and think as you do, and assess the situation through their lens.

They listen carefully and understand what you, their friend, went through, and how that made *them* feel. This is usually the technique psychologists follow, which is why they are able to help people.

- **Communication Ability**

While listening is a great virtue, being able to communicate is also an important pillar. All of us can open our mouths and blabber along, but how many of us can articulately convey what we have to say? Hence, your friend must be one who is able to communicate, in a few words, what they want to tell you.

- **Should Come from Experience**

You must have heard of this famous phrase, 'You will never understand one's journey unless you have walked in their shoes'? The best person to seek advice from will always be someone who has once been a DGP tormented by a CCB and then rose to defeat them.

When you know a person who has been through what you are going through now, your trust in them strengthens. It makes you feel more comfortable opening up to them. Consequently, it enables them to empathise with you and communicate the support.

- **Must Not Abuse Their Knowledge of You**

When you open yourself up to someone, you take a leap of faith. You believe that this person will respect your privacy and keep your secrets to themselves. However, it is always prudent to not entirely entrust a person with your story. Ensure that your friends will never, under no circumstances, betray or abuse their knowledge of you.

You must remember that you will be required to share everything with them. You will have to empty your soul to them. That is the only way for you to reorient your thought process, feelings, actions, language, and the various situations for you to stand up and fight.

All in all, these are the qualities you must look for in the person who can successfully guide you through your journey from a victim to a conqueror. This is not a one-time session and can take anywhere between weeks to years for you to make the transition. It boils down to how soon you can gain clarity about yourself and the situation and resume in the field without being affected by the CCB.

Only then will you see through the fog that has clouded your vision of the outside world, clouded your ability to take a stand against the CCB. If you can find people who reach out with a helping hand to pull you out of your past, by supporting you or encouraging you to seek help, do not let go of that grip. This is your way out.

Are you ready to take a CCB head-on?

Think it through

There are several ways for you to tackle a CCB. Though it may seem like there are too many options, you have to realise which one works for you, and for that to happen, you need to conduct an analysis. Without this, you will always be walking on thin ice.

Let's say you have arrived at the office today with the firm determination to speak up against the CCB's insults or humiliation. You will get cold feet in the beginning, which is only natural, but if you are not sure of what your approach is, if you cannot place your faith in the process that you have chosen, you will never be able to actually execute it.

Should you be locking horns with them aggressively, or should you confront them with a calm mind? You might want to reorganise the deal at that point and want to talk about the arrangement, so keep in mind that under no circumstances must you mince words.

You might want to maintain your tonality, etiquette, and be truthful while conducting the conversation in a respectful way. You see, there are a lot of things that you might be asking yourself. The question is, how prepared are you for the battle?

How do you begin?

Now, the best way to assimilate all your concerns would be to list them as bullets. You could write them down as fully formed sentences, but I believe that it wavers the concentration. Bullet points are a concise format that opens multiple areas for discussion. It brings many issues to light. This might take you by surprise initially, but you will work your way through it. After that, you can start underlining the things that really matter to you.

Practice by speaking out loud

Grab hold of a close friend, spouse, or partner and create a mock discussion. It will help you experience the discomfort and the emotions and teach you how to handle them. Speaking your argument out loud will also bring clarity to your thought process.

Record yourself on video. That way, you will be able to watch yourself later and correct your mistakes. However, this is just a suggestion; it does not necessarily mean that it will work for everybody, but there's no harm in trying it once.

You must remember to practice hands-free, that is, record yourself by placing the phone on a stand. This will make it more realistic, like you're actually talking to someone. Practice your way to find the fine balance between courage and consideration.

Remember that it might be really challenging for you to execute this plan at the first shot. It has been years since you have confronted the issue. Therefore, initiating the conversation will be your biggest hurdle. You may never find that perfectly scripted start.

You might start by saying, 'I want to talk to you about something', or take your shot when the conversation moves that way by saying, 'I've been wanting to talk to you about this'. Another alternative would be for you to tell them straight away, 'I disagree with you', when they impose an opinion on you.

No matter how you jump into it, the CCB will find something to pick on you about. They might try to derail the issue or retaliate by saying that you have killed the conversation, or blame you for 'overreacting'. I understand how difficult it might be for you to start the discussion with the person, knowing very well that you will be vilified; however, you must go through with it.

It might coerce you into becoming too soft, too demanding, or too firm, which goes against the wisdom of the books and theories that tell you to balance these three. I know that's not very easy to do. So, you go ahead, burn your hands, burn your fingers, but remember that, in the end, you will come out of this fight smiling and relieved. Then, the only questions you will have left to ask yourself will be, why didn't I do it sooner?

There is a very famous saying in Hindi, which goes along these lines—*Jab jago, tabhi savera.* (Whenever you wake up, that is when the morning starts.) Take your time because all that matters is that it results in your victory. When you start practising, you must keep in mind that there are several levels that you will be unlocking slowly as you move further.

Your initial goal is to be truthful and respectful. Hence, you start there. Slowly, you can start adding each aspect into the mix as you keep climbing up the levels. For example, in the next level, you can try being truthful, respectful, and flexible. Then, you can add humour. Finally, you can overtly assert your maturity and your wisdom in this situation.

If you feel that you're being selfish, remind yourself that this is about yourself. This is about self-care. It is not about anybody else; therefore, there is no way this situation can be turned around to your exhibition of selfishness.

When it comes to practising tonality, the easiest place for you to practice this in real life is with someone you are not close to, such as the waiter at a restaurant. I am not asking you to be mean with them; I am just telling you to practice honesty with them. When they ask you if you liked the food, instead of telling them you enjoyed it, irrespective of whether you actually liked it or not, you can convey your candid opinion.

This is your first step at practising boldness. This is you talking, and others listening. This is you strengthening your own spine because you will need it when you talk to the CCB.

7.2 Strategies and Tricks

Should you, as a DGP, let your guard down when your relationship with a CCB seemingly improves?

No. *Nahin.* Nada.

Absolutely not.

This is one of the biggest mistakes you can commit.

When you keep your guard up, it leaves little room for warmth, bonding, or cohesion. This creates a rigid and inflexible relationship, which makes it inhabitable for any kind of trust to blossom. Once the CCB is convinced that you are not a fool, that you are not gullible, that you cannot be manipulated or made into an easy target every time, and that you know when to say no, the question may arise as to whether you should try to recover the bond and trust you once shared with them.

Well, in such a case, two possibilities exist: A prospective friendship or the continuation of the existing rigid relationship. However, once a CCB pegs you as intelligent, the relationship does improve significantly, but does that mean you can take it absolutely easy now?

No.

Reasonably easy?

Yes.

Why?

Two reasons: one, because you know how to deal with them, and their behaviour does not affect you as much now. Two, they know you can see through them.

This new relationship might not host spontaneity, but it does include respecting each other's competence and intelligence. However, keep in mind that regardless of how much your relationship may seem to have improved, they are still a CCB. Hence, they will test you occasionally.

They might appear to be extra courteous, but the moment you let your guard down, they will attack you with all their force. Just because a CCB softens their stance and behaves themselves does not mean that you should drop your guard.

A CCB may come and tell you, "Let's trust one another," but you must know more than that and steer clear of these traps. Instead, let them invest in the relationship, let them make the first move, and then you reciprocate that. Again, do not go overboard with it.

DGPs crave warmth, sweetness, and amicable conversations due to their inherent intimacy vacuum. So, if you find the CCB showering extra attention on you, it is cause to worry. You may even find the CCB being vulnerable and sharing secrets with you. Does that mean you have to respond to the gesture by sharing your own?

NO!

You never know when they will revert to their old ways and start insulting you again. When something like this happens, you must be careful not to let it pass. Every time a CCB tries to violate the trust that you have built, make it loud and clear that you have not succumbed to their apparent niceties. Speak up. Every time.

Therefore, your job is going to be a little similar to that of a CCB's. You, too, will have to test people out before trusting them again. Sooner or later, under pressure or pleasure, their true character will reveal itself, and once you catch a glimpse of that, you are good to go. Go ahead and make a decision; should you trust them or should you not?

You will meet a lot of people in your life who will tell you that you must never be judgemental. What I am trying to tell you is that you should always judge people. Does that necessarily make you judgemental? Most certainly not. It makes you intelligent and more conscious about your choices. The words might sound similar, but there are marked differences.

You must not get emotional, but does that mean you should not have emotions? Absolutely not! You may have emotions and celebrate having them, but you never allow emotions to cloud your judgement. You must resolve to never let impure or confused emotions lead the way. Pure emotions are chastened by superior values, and they may provide you inspiration to act, and that is alright.

Human beings function with the coexistence of two factors: independence and integration. Every person wants to be independent—financially, socially, and emotionally. They want to be able to go wherever they want, do whatever they want whenever they want, and with whomever they want.

They don't want their decisions to be dependent on what another person thinks or wants them to do. On the other hand, every human being craves connection. Except for a very few, nobody can survive without being dependent on another person.

Sounds contradictory, doesn't it? Well, that's how we are – that is human civilisation for you. However, in order to find happiness, everybody needs to strike a fine balance between these two parameters. The best relationships are those where each partner offers the other an abundance of space and trust.

How do you get to that? Initiate a discussion. Communicate effectively.

As I have already mentioned, it is difficult to stay afloat in a conversation where the CCB only finds faults. Your job is to ensure that the slurs the CCB throws at you do not get under your skin. For that to happen, you have to practice aloud. In any case, a CCB will never make a conversation easy for you, but you must respond to the CCB with a rejoinder.

Let's say that the CCB has been exploiting you or the situation for a very long period – the longevity can range from anywhere between weeks and years.

What are the primary obstacles you face while confronting the CCB?

How do you kick off the discussion?

- After the inception of the conversation, what if the CCB scuttles the dialogue? What if they turn it around and begin crying, screaming, and blaming you? What if they mutilate the data?

- What if you do not have the answers to all the questions that are raised by the other person? You might have thought that you prepared well for the situation, but the CCB presents you with something more twisted in the form of riddles, and that takes you by surprise.

- What if they cut you off midway and start talking about something else? What if they don't pay attention?

What do you do?

While a CCB's skills lie in tackling, insulting, and belittling you, you have to develop your negotiation skills as well as network-building ability in order to battle with them fairly. Let's elaborate a little on the latter part first: network-building ability.

A DGP typically finds it difficult to differentiate between a connection and a network. This is due to the goodness, innocence, or ignorance of their heart, which believes that relationships should not be encashed. A connection is just a contact, you know. It could be anyone—an acquaintance or a friend.

However, a network is a person who could also be a connection, but the difference is that you don't shy away from doing business with them. With these people, you must be comfortable to say, 'I could do this for you, and you could do this for me'.

When I play tennis, we hire a coach to complete our team as a doubles partner. Now, the coach charges a fee, and the last person left on the court ends up paying for it. If they are a DGP, they might not raise any objection and quietly continue to pay the coach. If you are a little better than that, you might mention that you will pay today.

If you are the DGP, it would probably be difficult for you to raise this question. My advice would be to conquer the fear and be upfront about sharing the fees equally for the rest of the association.

Every relationship thrives on the give-and-take ratio, as you may have experienced. If you are the giver, it is important to clarify what you are giving and the reason for giving, as well as stipulate the framework for sharing future expenses. Does this make the situation sound too monetary? Yes, but in the long run, fairness will serve you well.

A fair negotiation establishes trust and an open, comfortable association between both parties. It is a great way to coexist and synergise. Therefore, it is good to feel comfortable negotiating without any awkwardness or shame, while enabling the other person to deal with you in a similar way.

Oftentimes, while handling a CCB, you will find them referring to their connections. They may or may not introduce you to them, but they will get your job done and expect you to return the favour. Therefore, a DGP should build an armoury of resources that can be called upon when the time arrives.

In the event that you are in trouble, your contacts will come to your rescue, and flaunting your networks in front of the CCB will only convey the amount of power you hold. They will know that you are not to be meddled with.

Confrontation: Should you stoop down to a CCB's level when confronting them?

Every DGP suffers from this dilemma. The question that arises is, 'Wouldn't that put me on the same level as them? Doesn't that contradict everything I believe?' Honestly, what other alternatives do you have? You can either sit and suffer, or you can rise above that.

The unfortunate part is that as a DGP, this is precisely what you have been attempting to do – to rise and raise your voice. But instead, you look the other way, seething inside to very explosive levels, praying for a solution and hoping it will miraculously fall in your lap.

- Should you stoop down to their level?

- Is responding to them actually stooping down to their level?

- What will happen if you actually stoop to their level?

To answer the **first** question, if you don't, then you will have to suffer their condemnation. If you do, then you lower yourself in your eyes as you feel that you are now treading the path of the evil and the wicked. A double-edged sword, isn't it? Another thing you will notice during your tug-of-war with the CCB is that it is extremely time-consuming and energy-draining, and you would rather invest yourself more productively.

The question to ask yourself here is, is productivity the real reason, or is it just an excuse to compensate for your inability to stand up to the CCB? Is productivity your defensiveness towards conflict avoidance?

How about, instead of avoiding the CCB, you learn the correct strategies and tricks that will equip you in managing them? Apart from saving your time and energy, it will help you preserve your sanity by making you feel empowered and emboldened.

To answer the **second** question – is responding to them actually stooping down to their level? I think this whole idea of 'stooping down to their level' is really misplaced. So, if someone abuses you, should you return the favour? You most certainly can and should. There are also other strategies you can employ, but before we get to that, let us unbundle and deconstruct the concept of stooping.

It refers to an act that you hate about a certain person but which you are engaging in. Since you detest the behaviour or attitude, you disrespect yourself for exhibiting the same. This is where the problem lies! The issue is that we focus too much on what we mirror, rather than on the thought process for the same.

It would work to your interest if, instead of lowering your standards, you concentrate on raising them. Your thoughts, then, will resonate with the following ideas.

"Tackling *adharma* is *dharma*. Tackling unrighteousness is righteousness."

Start by removing the guilt and shame from acting like they did. The CCB has insulted and humiliated you, and by quietly accepting this, you have condoned their actions. This, in itself, is committing grave injustice to yourself. If you can let it pass, good for you, but if it keeps bothering you, then you have to do something about it.

Now, doing something about it includes tackling *adharma*, performing self-care, which again is *dharma*, and discouraging destructive behaviour. Rewire your brain to embrace conflict as you progress in life. Conflict is always going to be there. Your solution must be accepting it, not avoiding it.

After you accept conflict, your mind will no longer label it as a problem, and this will help you rise above it and find a solution. You will be able to see through the person's inequitable behaviour. This is the difference between patience and suppression.

Patience is knowing that this is a passing phase. The CCB is probably going through a tough time in their life, and once they surmount that, the phase will pass. Hence, there is no point in confronting it. Thus, people make peace with patience. There will be times when you might not be able to tackle an issue, but you have to be honest about it and accept this.

Your solution must not lie in brushing it under the carpet and pretending as though it never happened. *That*, is where the problem begins. It might not affect you immediately, but it slowly creeps into your subconscious, and you begin fostering the emergence of a false self.

Should you continue a relationship with a CCB?

This is a difficult question to answer. The theoretical answer is yes, but in reality, it isn't always easy. What if the CCB is your child, partner, parent, friend, colleague, client, or somebody really close to you? What do you do?

Imagine an office filled with CCBs, but among all the people, you are the only one singled out for the suffering. Maybe you are a soft person; maybe you have been sending the wrong signals. You are not in a position to leave that job, which doesn't leave you with too many options. This happens to most people.

You cannot just go around severing ties. What you can do instead is modify the relationship you have with them. You can either distance yourself from them, or you could observe the situations or instances where they pick on you and ensure that you avoid such situations. That is to say, do not let any instance escalate to a position where you have to bear the brunt.

Pre-empting a CCB's moves

In most cases, CCBs possess a superior and sharper intellect, which makes it all about 'me' rather than 'we'. Their intelligence puts them in a powerful position, making them adept at breaking the rules or thinking several steps ahead of you. They have fun at your expense, playing a vicious cat-and-mouse game, which puts you under constant threat or attack.

It is impossible and insane to think that you can pre-empt the CCB's moves, as there is an incessant barrage of tantrums, difficulties, impediments, and obstacles that you will have to deal with.

However, there is light at the end of the tunnel— every time the CCB harasses you, note it down. When this has happened too many times, it will reveal a pattern.

Therefore, the next time something like that is about to happen, you will see the warning signs. This will give you extra time to take him by surprise, either by flaunting the name of a superior contact, or by building an army of allies around you to rally against him.

Better still, keep your gaze steadfast, look straight into his eyes, and smile as he keeps blabbering. If nothing else, this at least gives you the confidence that you can pull a move against them if you have to.

Handling a CCB is easier for some people

The more intelligent you are, the easier it is for you to handle a CCB. You are better at judging, observing, and analysing the CCB strategies. You are always on guard as you know that, no matter how pleasant the situation may be, the CCB can revert to being a snake at any time. You have clarity about what you want or what you do not want.

In order to say no, you must be sure of what you are saying yes to. Most DGPs crave love, warmth, and harmony, but they are also cognisant of the fact that achieving peace won't get them anywhere. Let us imagine that you would like to participate in the dance class today. You know what you want, and you also know what you do not want.

Your only requirement is to not just avoid conflict but also enjoy every bit of the time you spend there. Thus, if the teacher suddenly stops you from dancing, you will protest because you know what you are fighting for.

Or say, you want that seat on the flight. You were the first to enter, and that is why you should get it.

Now, what do you prefer? Harmony, absence of unpleasantness, pseudo-morality, or misplaced virtuosity? Or that particular seat because it has more legroom, and which you will fight for?

You need to have clarity about who you are and what you want. Only then will you be able to pay attention to those needs and work towards ensuring their fulfilment. This is called being in touch with yourself, loving yourself. Do not confuse self-care with selfishness. You are simply paying as much heed to yourself as you would to a loved one, and that is your right! You have to love yourself; that is how you have convictions; that is how you build spine.

Another parameter to factor in is courage. You could have built this up during your growing years, or it could have been nurtured in you since infancy, thanks to a strong, supportive family foundation. As a result, your real self is not enveloped by your false self. You are secure in your thoughts and your ways.

Insecure people find it difficult to gain clarity about anything as they have always lived under the garb of a false self. This makes it challenging for them to attune themselves to reality, so they simulate one for themselves, and their minds end up exaggerating everything.

Is there a clear answer to which fights one must pick up and which ones to let go? The answer is no. The people who advise you to 'pick your battles' never say which ones to choose. As a result, you could pick the wrong fight and let go of the less harmful ones. So, how do you learn? Where do you find a 'fight compass'?

You learn by analysing. You have to start by analysing yourself. Where do you stand in the four quadrants? Are you a Well-Intentioned Intelligent person, or are you a Well-Intentioned, Not So Intelligent person? As soon as you figure this out, you must categorise the CCB you are dealing with.

Experience is another factor that helps people manage CCBs. You have burnt your hands in the past; now, you're not going to let them see you anymore. You've reached a level where you can comfortably play their games and win too. Detachment plays a huge role here. When you know that you will be alright, even without the relationship, you are detached.

In no way am I referring to breaking off any relationship, but to the fact that you do not have a compulsive need for this relationship to exist. Your reaction should not reflect in any decision or action of yours. This one decision should not overwhelm you so much that you lose sight of everything.

Accept the fact that wherever you go, however you are, there will always be enemies. You have to be detached. You should be the one controlling your emotions; you should not let your emotions control you. If you are hypersensitive or hyper-emotional, do not worry. You will gradually develop a thick skin that will insulate you from the knocks and shocks of an unfair world.

Do you have a bad temper? If you want to be able to handle a CCB, better keep it in check. If a CCB angers you, chances are that you will react impulsively rather than intelligently. Exposing your temper is exposing a weakness, and that is your vulnerability. They will prey on this to bring you down. On the other hand, if you keep your head calm, your mind will present different ideas to handle the situation. That is when your intellect can operate at its best.

You can tell them 'better deal or NO deal'

In 90% of the cases, you will find that the CCB has a lot to gain from the DGP. When the DGP tries to talk it out rationally with the CCB, the latter endlessly confuses them with convoluted analysis, paralysis, and arguments. The CCB snubs them to avoid giving the DGP justice or good, honest collaboration.

When the CCB appears to be gaining a lot from the DGP, either by his exploitative or manipulative nature, the DGP can get back at them by saying, 'I do not want to transact with you' or 'I will transact with you, but only on my terms'. This could lead to a wonderful turn wherein the deal gets negotiated in their favour.

As a DGP, you unwittingly give so much of yourself and without compensation, but the moment you withdraw and put your terms on the table, you will get a far better deal. You can then celebrate and discover your own strength.

The correct word here is not 'drawing boundaries'; the correct word here is 'offering another deal'. So, you're saying, 'Either I do this deal or there is NO deal'.

Why is it more difficult to handle good-looking CCBs?

Many people have asked me this question; they find it extremely difficult to deal with the games good-looking CCBs play. It becomes difficult to draw boundaries or push back in that case. One of the greatest drawbacks is that when attractive people are good to you, it makes you feel good about yourself.

Their magnetic personality overwhelms you, and even something as small as a smile can prompt you to jump through hoops for them. You put yourself at such a subservient level that when this good-looking CCB abuses you, you are not able to muster up the courage to fight back.

If you begin to interact with a CCB without preparation, chances are that you will lose sight of your goal very quickly. A DGP colleague may work overtime to help an attractive CCB colleague in order to win brownie points and befriend them. The latter will continue to take favours without repaying any back.

When the DGP realises he or she has been used, instead of avoiding conflict with the attractive colleague, the DGP must acknowledge and accept the conflict. If you find yourself getting attracted to a person who seems to be taking advantage of you, watch out. Do not fall for this trap. Once aware of a situation like this, you will be better prepared to cope with it.

So, how do you protect yourself?

One: Be aware of the situation and accept any forthcoming conflict.

Two: Practice detachment. This one might be a bit difficult since it requires practice, but it is not impossible. I have discussed detachment earlier in this chapter.

7.3 Evaluating Progress

How do you know you are making progress in dealing with the CCBs?

This might sound vague, but the truth is that if you are really making progress, you will know. A tiny voice at the back of your mind will tell you that you have succeeded. These are all intuitions and feelings; let's take a look at the tangibles.

While it would be unfair to say that CCBs can *never* change, I can tell you that most of them choose not to. Hence, the only one progressing and rising above would be you. Now, even before a CCB humiliates you, you will be able to analyse their pattern. You will know what they're trying to do. And if you know that, then chances are you will be able to pre-empt their move.

A little later, you will find that presence does not bother you anymore; it does not compel you to respond to them. You won't find it necessary to defend yourself from them any longer. If they tell you that you need to prove yourself, you will just sit there and smile at them or walk away.

You will be comfortable with silence around them. You may even become better at counter-attacking. They may try to evoke a response by making offensive personal remarks, such as on your weight or appearance: "Oh, you've become fat. Looks like you have been making huge pots of money."

At such times, feel free to return the blow with a knockout punch, such as, "I'm fat because I socialise. Oh, but you wouldn't understand that—you have no friends."

It could lead to a fight, but more often than not, I have seen that when they attack you on personal attributes and you respond with an equally scathing rejoinder, they retreat. Sometimes, they will try to test you by escalating the fight, but you can always stay quiet and choose not to respond. This will show indifference. This will prove that you are detached.

As you improve your skills, you will no longer feel angry or bitter when you are mean to them. You will no longer think before retaliating because you know that they deserve it, and you are confident that you are doing the right thing.

Soon, you will get out of the toxic cycle of feeling shame or 'stooping low', where you continuously question yourself if you're doing the right thing. Play their game and win at it—when you see this happening, you will know that you have progressed.

CHAPTER 8

THE INFLUENCE OF TEACHERS, SCHOOLS AND SOCIETY

Empathy is one of the greatest qualities a human being can possibly possess. However, empathy, at the cost of not being able to honour your own emotions, is not so great. Several people become masters at empathy; they are given the badge of a 'good listener' from their friends.

They are always engaged in the process of understanding others' needs and wants because that is how they were programmed in their childhood. On the contrary, if you ask them if they are sympathetic towards themselves or if they are in touch with their feelings, you may get a blank look. Why does this happen? Because there is a hole in their soul that has never been filled up by anybody.

This discussion is going to be about how comfortable you are in your skin. One important thing to remember: emotional development does not necessarily happen because you intellectualise something. Knowing concepts like self-esteem, self-concept, or self-respect does not give you the ability to practice them.

Once you are admitted to school, you realise that now you can do things in a group. For the first time, you are introduced to the idea of teamwork. This is the space where you can play together, eat together, fight together, or even share your work. However, along with cooperation comes conflict.

Each of the people you make friends with is different. Each of them comes from a different background, which also makes their emotional personalities unique from one another. You will be faced with the challenge of dealing with inter personality conflicts or expression.

Now, let us take a look at the influence our teachers, schools, and society have on us.

Influence of teachers

Teachers have a profound and long-lasting influence on all of their pupils. This influence includes not only the teaching of specific academic skills, but also, and perhaps more significantly, the development of students' self-esteem. Self-esteem reinforcement in the classroom has been linked to improved motivation and learning.

How Teachers Encourage Self-esteem

Teachers need to understand and consciously employ techniques to promote self-esteem, along with their focus on imparting academic skills. An emphasis on self-esteem, on the other hand, will also help build a more exciting and rewarding teaching atmosphere. Teachers' sensitivity, respect, and care, rather than financial costs or budget, are needed for self-esteem strategies.

Some of these self-esteem strategies can include making students feel like they are welcome and belong in the school setting, giving them responsibilities that enable them to feel like they are contributing and making a difference (e.g. tutoring younger children, helping to care for school plants), and giving them opportunities to make choices and decisions and solve problems. Although positive approaches are important for all students, they are especially important for students who struggle with learning.

In retrospect, many adults harbour bad memories of instances where they thought teachers demeaned, belittled, or accused them of being disruptive simply because they were unable to understand what was being taught. Children with learning disabilities are particularly susceptible to this type of treatment, and sadly, even today, are labelled as lazy, unmotivated, or distracted and are coerced into paying more attention and asking fewer questions.

Actually, teachers must continually convey to students that making mistakes is part of the learning process and that no student should ever be afraid to ask questions if they do not comprehend a topic.

Acknowledge the Fear of Failure

To reduce students' fear of making mistakes and feeling embarrassed, I recommend that on the first or second day of the new school year, teachers ask students, "Who thinks they would possibly make a mistake in class this year, or not understand anything the first time?"

And before anyone replies, the teachers must raise their own hands. Teachers should then ask the class why the question was asked and use student responses as a springboard to explore how the fear of not understanding anything and making mistakes interferes with expressing their thoughts or attempting an answer, even if it is wrong.

Indian society, unfortunately, is intolerant of failure and aspires to seek perfection, which is near-illusionary. On the other hand, recognising and expressing one's fear of failure reduces its potency and ability to destroy the emotional self.

Teachers should never underestimate the impact they have on the lives of their students. Rather than just focusing on the lesson of the day, they should aspire to become a 'charismatic adult' who has the power to not only touch their students' minds but also their spirit. They should be positive influencers who reinforce positive emotions. Such power is a precious right that should be cherished and nurtured.

Teachers Can Truly Change Lives

We know that a great teacher has the power to change a student's life; some of us may have even experienced this blessing! There are countless stories that testify to the value of a strong relationship between an educator and a student. Teachers, as some of the most important role models for student development, are responsible for more than just academic enrichment.

To be a great educator, you must communicate with your students and meet them on many levels because the best teachers care for their students' well-being, both inside and outside of the classroom. Educators can influence practically every aspect of their students' lives by developing good relationships with them and teaching them critical life lessons that will help them excel beyond term papers and standardised tests.

It is not always easy to change a student's life, which is why a great teacher is needed. Some students just need a little extra encouragement, such as the student whose math grade is only a few points short of the A that will earn them a 4.0 GPA; others may be going through a difficult time in their personal lives and need someone to speak to. A life-changing teacher must be able to provide whatever assistance the student requires to succeed.

Influence of school

Ideally, the school's job is to help each student reach his or her full academic potential. While the efficacy varies from school to school, simply teaching the ABCs and 123s isn't enough. A considerable amount of schoolwork is devoted to assisting children in becoming expert problem-solvers and solution-seekers, skills that will come in handy in almost every personal and professional area of a child's adult life.

People with a problem-solving mentality seek out challenges because they realise that resolving difficulties helps reduce the number of obstacles they face. They see problems as opportunities to improve rather than as traumatic experiences. However, a person or a child can only develop a functional problem-solving mindset if they have, without any obstacles, developed the emotional self.

To put it simply, they need to feel safe in order to approach a problem. Most happy and inventive problem-solvers come from families where a healthy environment was practised and encouraged. On the other hand, you will notice that people who have a less than fulfilling emotional development do their best to avoid a problem.

They develop an 'avoiding instinct', i.e. contrary to solving the problem, they will steer away from it. Therefore, a problem solver has an engaging instinct, and a problem avoider has an evading instinct.

As a result, problem-solving is a necessary life skill in addition to an academic skill. It is the ability to evaluate a problem, formulate a solution, and if that solution fails, re-strategise to try again. The problem-solving mindset inspires children to keep trying, even though they fail the most recent math exam. They will press on and persist because the mindset still dictates that there is a solution; it has just not been discovered yet, and that appears to be the problem.

Social Skills

Being the class topper is of no value in the real world if the child lacks the healthy social skills to complement it. He/she won't be able to pass their first job interview, and they'll most likely be spending weekends alone on the couch with the television and a bag of chips for company. The school is critical in teaching children how to communicate favourably with their peers and teachers. They learn about positive communication skills and further improve them through experiences in the classroom and on the playground.

A child's emotional and social maturity serves as the foundation for all other aspects of his or her growth. When educators disregard children's emotional and social growth, it frequently results in adults who are academically gifted but struggle in their daily lives due to a lack of self-esteem and/or social skills.

Children spend a significant portion of their day at school, so it is critical that a school's curriculum is tailored to help students develop strong social relationships, or interact with other children and adults in a caring, empathetic, and authentic manner—so that they nourish themselves while nurturing relationships around them.

Concept of Self

Now that the child is earning straight A's and has landed his/her first job, it's time to concentrate on character and values. Character development is not an alternative to academic achievement, but rather a necessary complement to it. In addition to teaching reading, writing, and arithmetic, the school from the start must focus on teaching children values such as self-compassion, respect, empathy, and honesty.

It starts with simple lessons like raising your hand to talk and keeping your hands to yourself. It eventually evolves into argumentative debates on moral and social problems. By the time the child graduates from high school, he should have a good understanding of his own principles, values, and self-image.

If he believes he is a poor communicator, he is unlikely to seek a career in law or public speaking. This understanding of who he is and what he values will guide his academic, professional and personal endeavours.

Participation in New Activities

A child's school will expose him or her to a wide range of opportunities. Children are often exposed to various nationalities, cultures, and customs from an early age, which helps form their perspective of the world around them. Field trips and interactive projects enable them to try new things, and each subject gives them a preview of what they can expect in the future.

A range of extracurricular activities, including joining the swimming team, volunteering to work with younger children, running for the post of school treasurer, and competing to lead the chess club, can help shape their interests, self-esteem, and the trajectory of their academic and professional life.

If a child goes through all of these activities with a well-developed emotional self, these activities not only become enjoyable but also help to expand their consciousness, awareness, circle of influence, and engagement with life. When one engages in all these activities from the place of a true self, then one does not suffer from the disease of perfectionism, anxiety, or envy.

Instead, the experiences become a celebration, and failures become learnings. When the emotional self is developed or is developing in the right direction, then we do not self-criticise ourselves excessively and do not have fears of abandonment and toxic shame.

Influence of society

There is a substantial body of evidence to prove that a person's social environment affects their health status, though the mechanisms which lead to this are yet to be understood. For instance, it has been theorised that youngsters may mimic what they find in their current circumstance.

Therefore, the individuals who experienced childhood in settings characterised by top-notch education and childcare, get access to a range of essential services, sporting facilities, and social cohesion, over those who experienced childhood plagued by constant social threats and a lack of resources.

The social climate of a child is primarily determined by where their parents live and where they are schooled. As many of the relationships children create are within their family or neighbourhood, the social environment has a large influence on who they form relationships with and the nature of the relationships.

As a result, the parents' decisions (or, conversely, lack of decision-making power) on where to live, work, and go to school may significantly impact their children's health and well-being. The social environment of a child has an effect on their cognitive growth and educational achievements.

Children who participate in positive social interactions outperform those who do not. Children who live in social settings with residential stability are less likely to miss school and do better academically than those who do not. Those who live in lower-income neighbourhoods are more likely to drop out of school than their more affluent counterparts.

Early childhood education is where a child forms social relationships with other children and teachers, while also developing pro-social behaviour, which has an especially profound impact on potential academic achievement. Pre-schoolers outperform their peers academically and are less likely to repeat a grade.

There is evidence that the social environment influences cognitive growth during early childhood, even if a child later moves to a different neighbourhood. A child who grows up in a low-income neighbourhood, for example, may have poor cognitive growth and academic results, even if they move to a wealthy neighbourhood later in life.

There is also an intergenerational influence, and children whose parents grew up in deprived neighbourhoods have poor cognitive growth and educational achievement even if they grow up in a more prosperous neighbourhood.

Taking Decisions on an Impulse

Growing up in a healthy social setting has been linked to lower chances of impulsive behaviour. Children who grow up in a positive setting are less likely to have injuries that necessitate medical attention than those who do not. Children who have healthy social interactions have a lower chance of having a drug use disorder than those who do not.

Sense of Belonging

An individual's mental well-being benefits from the sense of belonging they feel when they have healthy social connections. Children who have positive social relationships have higher self-esteem than those who do not, and they are less likely to suffer from mental health issues, such as depression and anxiety. There is also evidence that pro-social behaviour in adolescence contributes to improved adult psychological well-being.

The social environment may also have an effect on a child's well-being by affecting their parents' behaviour. For example, Australian research found that parents in more open communities were less likely to use aggressive parenting strategies, which are supposed to have harmful psychological effects on their children, than those in less accessible communities.

Nature vs nurture has always been a debate. My personal view is that both factors play an equally important part in determining the future of the child. To decide whether he or she will grow up to become a CCB as a defence mechanism for survival, or submit to his or her weakness and find comfort in becoming a DGP, where the blame can always be passed on to another.

CHAPTER 9

SOME INTERESTING DISCUSSIONS

9.1 Common Questions and Thoughts About CCBs

In the process of reading this book, I am sure many questions may have cropped up in your mind. Let me answer some of them.

Is it acceptable to call bad people bad?

Well, if we are to follow in the footsteps of our forefathers, the answer would be yes. Several religious texts, especially the *Bhagavad Gita*, strongly call out bad people. Chapter 16 calls bad people demonic and good people divine. However, if you suffer from misplaced virtuosity and pseudo-morality, you will think otherwise. You will find excuses and reasons to justify their behaviour.

To answer the question, it is perfectly acceptable and human to call a person out for their bad behaviour.

Do bad people have the capability to become good people?

This is one of the most important questions I would like to address in this book. I have discussed CCBs and DGPs in separate chapters, and now I will talk about the journey a CCB can make to become a DGP if they wish to. Before I jump into that, we will have to understand the concept of devolutionary people and evolutionary people.

Devolutionary people and evolutionary people

Evolutionary people are those who are in a perpetual journey of self-development. This does not mean that they lead an unhappy life, but a constructive fire in their belly motivates them to seek higher levels of joy.

Evolutionary people constantly swim upstream in anticipation of self-improvement or to make something better. They are always looking to enhance or embellish a quality or a skill. As a result, they view weaknesses in their character, competence, and communication under a microscopic lens and focus on improving them.

Their goal is to become a virtuous person and attain higher values. Now, if you try to deconstruct what higher values necessarily stand for, then you'll find that these are values that have more longevity and universality to them.

For example, honesty has lifelong benefits. It grounds you; it makes you feel anchored. An evolutionary person would always want to live a life that is virtuous, and irrespective of what their true nature is, their effort would always be towards self-enhancement.

Let us say, I have a selfish friend who manipulates his wife, children, parents, and every other person who loves him dearly.

But when he talks to me, he is just a normal guy who is trying hard to resist this part of his persona. Every time we meet, he asks me for a solution. He wants to let go of this dark side and become a better person. There, you see, is that evolutionary streak I have been talking about.

A person cannot be deemed evolutionary based on their current personal traits, but on whether there is a willingness to rise above these qualities, redeem themselves, and invest the effort to become an improved person. It is all about the direction one takes—evolutionary direction or the devolutionary. It is not your willpower, but which direction you exert your willpower towards, and I say this from experience.

I have met several people who are lazy and crooked, and some of them even acknowledge this. Some are helpless, while others deliberately engage in such behaviour, but the common thread that binds them together is a deep desire to resist that negativity. Now, negating these things doesn't make you a good person overnight.

It could mean that if the person has been detrimental to another's confidence, he will attempt to mend his ways by learning to be more compassionate and empathetic, and eventually eradicate the harm he is causing to himself and to the other.

So, what does evolutionary mean? It means that you have an uphill battle, but you are not necessarily a restless ball of energy. Evolutionary people will always try to improve themselves, but that does not classify them as self-improvement junkies. It only means that you will no longer seek ways and means to justify your stored negativity.

How Does One Become Evolutionary?

By including and being committed to certain values, such as being honest, sympathetic, compassionate, collaborative, or having the courage to fight against injustice, this would enable them to strike a fine balance between courage and consideration, to marry paradoxes, and to develop wisdom.

These are only some of the qualities a person can inculcate in themselves to feel more stable and enjoy life at its finest. It helps them steel themselves against the bullets of life. They understand their feelings and are able to process them better. They become weatherproof; they could have an eternal summer or a freezing winter, yet they would be able to celebrate life. This is evolution, when you become the master of your inner and outer world.

You become aware of your thoughts, emotions, and get comfortable with them. You accept your true nature. When you finally become evolutionary, you stop being excessively critical of yourself or of others. Thus, evolution is everything that evolves you a little bit, promotes *Sattva*[30] in you, and takes you closer to the inner active silence inside of you.

---

[30] In Sanskrit, "Sattva" generally translates to "goodness", "purity", "truth", or "existence". It is also one of the three fundamental qualities (gunas) in Hindu philosophy, along with rajas (passion) and tamas (inertia), describing the nature of reality and the human psyche.

Imagine a scenario where an abusive mother-in-law justifies her actions towards her daughter-in-law under the guise of family traditions. This is something that a true devolutionary person would do because deep down, when your conscience says that this is not the right thing to do, but you use all the excuses to justify it and promote that activity, you're not being evolutionary, are you? You're not resisting your natural path of abuse with people and leveraging your strength and resources for your benefit.

Now, What is Devolutionary, You Ask?

If something prods you towards becoming selfish, it is devolutionary. If you constantly find yourself agitated, not being able to get love, give love, or be comfortable with yourself, you are taking a devolutionary step. If you see that you are always a step away from attacking someone or giving in to impulses just for the sake of your ego, you might have already devolved a bit.

The devolutionary person constantly focuses on serving their own ego and fulfilling their desires, and in the process, strangulating themselves. As a result, the devolutionary person will have more enemies as they will always try to play a win-lose game. However, the primary focus must not be the actions of the devolutionary person, but their intention.

The thought process of a devolutionary person starts and ends with *I, me, myself*; *I* will attack you; *I* will grab from you; *I* will cheat you; *I* will demean you. To them,

'I' supersedes 'you'. I hope this clarifies the difference between an evolutionary and a devolutionary person.

In Chapter 16, the Bhagavad Gita speaks of something similar. The question pertains to the ability of a devolutionary person to become an evolutionary person. Can they steer the course of their life in a different direction—can they change themselves? In my existence of more than five decades on this planet, I haven't come across many people who are pursuing evil, turning towards good. Does that make me a pessimist?

What I'm trying to say is that it is very difficult for a person's fundamental character to change. When a person has become, by nature or nurture, ill-intentioned, then it is not so easy for them to become well-intentioned.

I have seen some people change when they have had children; however, that is not necessarily true in every case. I know of enough people who continue to be ill-intentioned towards their children, as well as their parents.

Here, I take the opportunity to point out the difference between being self-centred and self-caring. Many people are under the misconception that if you take time for yourself and make an effort to take care of yourself, it makes you a selfish person. Selfishness is when a person says, "I will cheat you, I will put you down, and I will do whatever it takes to fill up my void."

When a person practices self-care, their thought process is, 'I won't let you stop me from having a decently good life. I won't let you prey on me. I am not harming anybody, and I have a right to live the way I want'. Now, this is self-care; being confident about what you want is self-care.

However, that does not mean that an evolutionary person will always be in self-denial. Selfishness comes at the cost of others, whereas self-care is equivalent to taking care of yourself while protecting your inner being. It primarily requires you to protect yourself from those who don't want you to do that.

Suppose you and your friends are planning to dine out. They want Italian, but you feel like Indian. With your friends, you have a comfort level to do what you want. Sometimes you even settle for a compromise and tell yourself that these are your friends, and you can do this for them.

Then, when you go back, you realise you spent the same amount of money as them, but you did not have as much fun as them. Why is that? Why is it always you who has to put aside something in order to ensure that there is no negative energy around?

Now, what I talked about here is self-denial. This is what you must steer clear of. Instead, what you may want to practice is self-care. Many times, when you are assertive in a situation like this, you will find yourself asking questions like, "Am I doing something wrong?" No, you're not. There is nothing wrong about being assertive.

So, to answer the question, do people change from devolutionary to evolutionary?

Yes, but few.

Do they change when they conceive children, or when they fall in love with someone?

Maybe.

Can you cause a person's intention to change?

I think it is possible, but you can only bring about that change if you exhibit it around them constantly. That is, to become their role model, you would have to set an example for them to learn from you. If you simply dole out instructions, chances are you will be ignored. On the other hand, when you show them how beneficial it is and how important it is to practice evolution, they will take heed.

Coming back to the context of CCBs. Do they change, become constructive people, or stop abusing their intellect? There is no denying that CCBs are one of the most intelligent beings and have incredible foresight. I believe that if they played chess, they would excel at it. Why? Because they can pre-empt the next 6 or 7 moves simply by assessing the current situation.

I think one of the most powerful ways to get CCBs to change themselves is by showing them empathy. However, when I think about it, I believe that it must be pretty difficult for a CCB to resist abusing the world, considering the power they possess. Only the powerless would want to sermonise them on becoming constructive.

At the same time, if you give a DGP access to all that power, would they also turn into a crook, creep, or a bully? Should you give it a try and find out? My advice would be to avoid anything of that sort. You must live a life of evolution yourself and protect yourself from the CCBs. If they want to change their direction, they will do so on their own.

What if your child is a CCB? Like I've mentioned already, you can try to be a role model and practise the four strategies of the four quadrants that have been covered in the first two chapters of this book.

Coming back to the main question, can CCBs become DGPs? I honestly think this is too much of an ask. They do lead a comfortable, conscience-free life after all, albeit at somebody else's expense.

"One day, the CCB will realise that this is wrong," words spoken by a DGP. It is very difficult for a person, in this case, a CCB, not to abuse their power when they have the muscle. If you want the best seat on the bus, you'd be willing to break the queue for it.

There's another important thing that I must address: does using your power or using your connection to break a queue make you a CCB? No, not necessarily. Knowingly damaging other people for your benefit is one of the biggest characteristics of a CCB. However, there is a possibility that the DGP may also use their contacts to jump the queue for his vaccination. It works both ways.

I've seen very little change in a CCB, even if the intent is there. It may happen for a while, but it doesn't last too long. For example, when you fall in love or start a new job, you may try to tap into your CCB nature to protect yourself from getting hurt. Gradually, it catches up and becomes a part of your nature. Characters are very difficult to change.

Yes, the only time change could possibly happen is when you begin to live with a person who is above all of this—a *Satvik*. They are above the binaries of good and bad, justice and mercy, decent and shameless. They are not impacted by anything, and that is why they cannot be abused by a CCB. They live a higher life and will not be trapped in the pettiness of the CCB.

Thus, if a CCB lives with a boss, spouse, or sibling like this, there is a slight possibility of them dropping their guard in the assurance that this *Satvik* person is not out to get them. In the outside world, the CCB never loosens up; they are always on high alert. On the other hand, the *Satvik* is untouched by events and content in their world—all the qualities that a CCB does not have but may aspire to have, which could inspire them to change.

If the CCB has quietly swum upstream with the intention to change, the result could be evident in the right atmosphere. Let me illustrate with some examples.

In the literary masterpiece *Les Misérables*, when the thief is caught with the candles stolen from the cathedral and brought back to the priest, the latter says, "No, I gave it to him." He teaches the thief that life is about giving and not taking. It turns out to be a turning point in the life of the thief, who later accomplished great things.

This demonstrates that change can happen in an instant, but I personally do not agree with this. In my view, a person has to go through immense soul-searching before he becomes a changed man or woman. In the story, the thief battled with many negative decisions that compelled him to break the cycle, but he resisted those. Why?

Because, at that moment, he received unconditional love from the priest. There would have been an intense internal turmoil preceding the change, which appeared to be sudden.

Even Valmiki[31] did not transform into a priest from a bandit overnight. If we dig deeper, we may find that he was a good bandit who wasn't unfair to his fellow bandits, or maybe he was a good family man and this was simply his profession to feed their mouths.

The bad news is, the CCBs may never change. Therefore, as a DGP, you must know that you can't endlessly hope that the CCB will have a *hriday parivartan* (change of heart) someday. The only chance they have at changing from devolutionary to evolutionary, or from a CCB to DGP, is if they are in the company of people who set an example with their good values.

Take Revenge or not: To be or Not to be

If the question concerns the morality of revenge, then the obvious answer is that it is a bad thing to do. Or so say the

---

[31] Maharishi Valmiki - a name that inspires transformation and devotion. Once known as Ratnakar, a dacoit who lived a life of crime, he transformed into a sage through the teachings of Narad Muni.

people who give us clichéd wisdom, who preach morality and virtuosity. There's an often-quoted statement that goes around: Forgive and forget. But is it really practical to follow?

Imagine a person who has been consciously and deliberately unfair to you on several occasions and caused you grave emotional and mental distress. This has hurt you, and that hurt has turned into anger. How do you appease this rage? You want to get even with them; you want to feel vindicated.

But you know very well that revenge is regarded as bad or evil, as stooping down to the level of that person who committed the initial crime. If you give in to revenge once, it will compel you to continue until the scores are settled.

Or, gradually, after developing a lot of courage, conviction, and your own sense of philosophy, you may feel empowered to put yourself on par with the CCB, if not be stronger than them. Now, this can create a dilemma; will you find recourse and release the toxicity that has built up inside you by being vengeful and settling scores, or would you be better off by adopting a mindset of forgiving and forgetting?

If we were to look at this whole thing without an emotional, judgemental, or moralistic lens, then it is imperative to find out why the person wants to take revenge at all. One theory could be that revenge provides a sense of justice, or a sense of fairness to them, and is the only solution to calm their restlessness.

Now, when there is a desire for fairness, or if I put it crudely, an eye for an eye, they develop an inevitable need to feel rested or settled. If you feel that justice has been served when you settle scores, how does it make you feel? Does it create more hatred inside you, or does it lull you to sleep with a sense of calmness?

To answer this, I would like to introduce three categories of people who have been classified according to their mental texture. This is simply to help you structure your revenge tactics. Should your revenge be constructive or destructive? Will it fill you with peace or fuel further hatred? Should you be signing a peace treaty, or should you be settling scores? Depending on whether you are *Rajsik, Tamsik, or Satvik,* you will find your answer.

1. Tamsik:

This is the first category, which I've labelled as *Tamsik.* The word *Tamsik* is derived from the word *tamas,* which translates to a sense of indolence or a sense of understanding everything oppositely. They are thick-skinned, and that is why nothing touches them. They are known to see a simple thing as a convoluted version of something else.

For example, a lazy person will define it as restfulness. Similarly, a promiscuous person would term it as progressiveness and would even go to the extent of perceiving friendship as an area of entitlement.

For Tamsik people, the advice should be: you should let the past stay in the past. If you give the Tamsik person the freedom to do something about it, chances are they will do more damage than reap the benefits that could come out of a confrontation.

2. Rajsik:

The second category of people is the opposite of *Tamsik*. They are highly active, but there is a catch. With their activeness comes intense agitation. They are constantly caught up between opposites. For instance, when they try to achieve peace, they lose prosperity, or when they try to achieve prosperity, they lose peace. They are also not able to see things for what they are.

Rajsiks react differently. They might find happiness in prosperity for some time, but when they get beaten and bruised in its quest, they seek the peace of vacations. Then, as the comfort of the peace soaks them in, they begin to yearn for the assurance that comes from wealth. Thus, it is a vicious cycle.

Rajsiks shuttle between binaries. One would not say they shy away from hard work, but they remain confused most of the time. They are characterised by action and agitation. What should you do when you are dealing with a *Rajsik* CCB? As *Rajsik* CCBs are on a continuous journey of evolution, my advice would be to let bygones be bygones and focus on protecting yourself from CCBs in the future.

You could confront the CCB and talk about the injustice committed to you to get it out of your system. This way, the CCB cannot think that they have fooled the nice *Rajsik* or taken them for a ride. If this works out well, then it would be a relief to the *Rajsik* person.

3. Satvik:

The third category comes with a sense of poise and is easily able to transcend the dilemma of binaries. They are blessed with a sense of serenity, which helps them rise above these opposites and view them with perspective. These are the people who can follow most of the motherhood statements quite calmly.

According to a *Satvik*, toxicity is nothing but detrimental and, to an extent, irreversible, as the event that caused it has happened in the past. This is their take on revenge. What you have to ensure is that you do not let the incident happen in the future because hate only begets hate. That is why, if you are planning to take revenge on a *Satvik* person, it is pointless.

Build the relationship with a constructive approach, but keep your guard while dealing with delicate matters with the person who has been either a crook, creep, or bully in the past. You should always be calculated, but that does not mean that you would lose your sense of calmness or associate any sort of negative emotions with it.

Now, you may ask the question, how can the *Satvik* make a mistake? The truth is, to err is human. All in all, with the '*Satvik*' people, you can move on.

Revenge is a natural feeling, and whether it is right or wrong is a subjective matter. Revenge is about seeking justice for oneself. Many people are not able to forgive and forget. My advice to them would be to go settle the scores, to get your sense of fairness, but also be prepared for the consequences that it may further lead to.

You should also consider the possibility that this will be considered disgraceful by some people. If you have the *Sattva*[32], if you want to transcend the past, then that is the best option. If you do not have it, the least you can do is try to resolve it. It goes without saying that you should not do anything that you will regret for the rest of your life or something that could land you in jail.

So, is revenge a good thing or a bad thing?

I think it could work out well for the *Rajsik* and not so well for the *Tamsik*. The question will not arise in the case of the *Satvik*. If you are plotting revenge for a traumatic incident, be mindful of the fact that engaging in a discussion about the same will unleash painful memories and emotions.

Therefore, if you still insist on settling scores, my advice would be to do so only if you are in a position of emotional strength. A friend of mind Pavan once said

---

[32] Satya is a virtue in Indian religions, referring to being truthful in one's thought, speech and action.

that the countries which have not shed blood for the cause of justice have not developed character. I genuinely believe that to be true. If there is cruelty and wickedness in our boardrooms, one must fight back because without drawing boundaries, non-violence is often perceived as a sign of weakness.

Will Karma and Cosmos punish the Crooks, Creeps and Bullies?

The decent good people who have suffered at the hands of crooks, creeps, or bullies often believe that karma will punish their oppressors and God will take care of the rest. They often say, "wait and watch." The bully keeps advancing his career, grows his wealth, gets a good night's sleep, and all you do is keep waiting for karmic justice.

You keep waiting for God to punish him, but how many times do you see him get punished? I'll answer that for you. Rarely. Even then, we can never be sure whether it is karma or the randomness of the world that has played out. You'll see the CCB prospering, thriving, and surviving so much better than you. So, the question remains, will they get punished by the cosmos, or is the whole thing really a chaos?

A CCB may suffer because of their incompetence for not being able to follow the rules of the game, but they are often smart enough to avoid being called out. Waiting for karmic retribution or karmic justice is not a very empowering idea. You must not make illogical assumptions, since that could only point to your weakness.

When you say, "Let the cosmos take care of it," you are also saying that you are letting go of the whole thing. You will be letting go of the whole cause-and-effect thing, but you are still hopeful of retribution.

I have seen people pin their hopes on visualisation, and while I have nothing against such mystical faiths, they have only further strengthened my belief in the power of intellect, action, and reason. So, my suggestion would be to drop the magical assumption that Karma is going to strike them with lightning. Stop fooling yourself and develop the strength to do it yourself.

9.2 Can There Be CCB Nations, Cultures, and Communities?

I am asked this question a lot. Can the title of a CCB only be given to an individual, or can it extend to nations, cultures, or communities? Before I answer this, I would like to clarify that I am neither a sociologist nor an anthropologist. I am sure that there have been several studies conducted on this, but in my experience, I have not come across any so far.

I have travelled to around 40 countries and have conducted workshops in 30 of them. I must be honest; I have found each of them to be a stark contrast against another. I have found a lot of cultures to be aggressive, some to be collaborative, and others to be submissive.

I have come across certain countries that consider it smart to be a CCB. If you have that killer instinct, if you have it in you to be aggressive and attacking, then it is an attribute that commands respect.

Now, I know that there are certain jobs that demand this trait, which is why I would like to clarify that a winning or aggressive mindset does not always make one a CCB.

9.3 What Does a World Without CCBs Look Like?

Impractical.

Have you heard of Yin and Yang[33]?

There is good, and then there is bad, but that's not where it ends—there is bad in good, and then there is good in bad. Good cannot exist without bad. If there wasn't darkness, then you would never know light. Similarly, the world exists only because there are binaries.

Hence, to answer the question, a world without CCBs cannot exist. The world is made of positive and negative polarities. It will have justice and mercy, but it will also have leadership and followership, smartness and simplicity, and cruelty and kindness. Therefore, if it has DGPs, it is bound to have CCBs.

---

[33] Yin and yang represent a fundamental concept in Chinese philosophy, symbolizing two interconnected and complementary forces that are in constant interaction and balance. Yin is often associated with passivity, and femininity, while yang represents light, activity, and masculinity.

READINGS & REFERENCES

A good *shishya/disciple/mentee* must express gratitude and pay homage to his or her *gurus/teachers*. In the writing of this book, I have had many gurus inspiring me and showing me the path. Here are some authors and their work that have influenced me while writing this book.

1. The Mahabharata translated by Bibek Debroy (Volumes 1 to 10)

2. Homecoming: Reclaiming and Healing Your Inner Child by John Broadshaw

3. The Drama of the Gifted Child by Alice Miller

4. Vedanta Treatise: The Eternities by Swami Avula Parthasarathy

5. My Gita by Devdutt Pattanaik

6. The Supreme Yoga: Yoga Vasistha, by Swami Venkatesananda

7. In Woods of God Realisation by Swami Rama Tirtha

8. Bhaja Govindam by Adi Shankaracharya

9. Iron John by Robert Bly

10. Embracing Our Selves by Hal Stone and Sidra Winkelman

11. Facing Codependence by Pia Melody

12. Purva Mimansa Sutras by Jaimini Rishi

13. Devon Ke Dev—Mahadev (TV Series)

14. Visit to temples in Cambodia

MORE DISCLAIMERS

This is a dangerous book

A lot of you may feel that things have happened to you unfairly. You have tolerated a lot, which has led you to where you are today; scared of tackling the consequences of engaging with CCBs. There is no doubt that it *really* can be quite dangerous, as this could cost you your money, peace of mind, and maybe even your health could be at risk.

If you do not handle it well, it is going to be a problem for you, but if you happen to think on your feet and stand your ground, you will be heavily rewarded. The disclaimer for you would be that you have to be very careful while experimenting. You have to calculatingly plan every incident beforehand.

Let's say that you want to talk to your parents about a certain behaviour that you have found to be quite damaging for you—be it psychologically, physically, or even financially. Now, when you prepare yourself to talk to them, remember that the conversation may not be in your favour, and they might refute the whole theory, ascribing it to a figment of your imagination.

The very problem for which you sought a solution might go against you, so be prepared with your arguments in advance, or else it will be a very dangerous exercise.

What do you do?

This is what the book will help you with, and once it does, all of this will become relatively simpler.

Follow the models in the book. Find a confidante who will support you and help you conduct mock interviews. You can practice your reactions or expressions while you are alone, or sometimes practising with people also helps. Write down all the legible responses you believe you will receive from the other side. It will help you to come up with different ways to tackle them while enabling you to understand the extent you can push yourself to.

My purpose behind including this portion is just to alert you to look out for danger. It won't help you if you think that reading the book is all the preparation you need to engage with CCBs. They will never make it easy on you. To them, it will be a negotiation you lost.

The book will hold different meanings for different people

A CCB will understand the book differently than a *Tamsik*[34] person, and that is only natural. Some people may realise that it is wise to rationalise a situation under any circumstances. Now, rationalising may also include *rationaLIES*, i.e. lies that sound rational; that is to say, they may lie about a certain thing and try to rationalise how they are being fair.

---

[34] A tamasic nature is one that is lacking in motivation, clarity, and will.

What I am trying to say is that every book stands a chance of being misused, and this one is no exception. When you see something similar happening to you or in front of you, you must immediately call their bluff. This book is filled with illustrative models, concepts, and strategies which can be used, abused, and put to use for an unjust advantage. Be conscious and avoid stepping into a similar trap.

ABOUT THE AUTHOR

Yadhav Mehra is a leading international behavioural skills trainer and a critical-life-skills coach, who delivers high-energy, practical, empowering, motivational sessions, and keynote presentations that focus on the often-unspoken matters in the corporate world and in life. His strategies are honest and practical, empowering organisations to unleash the untapped potential of employees, enabling them to make an influential impact in the world.

His theories do not follow any rule book; they are simple philosophies that evolve from practical experience, and this is what makes them real and practical. That is why he prefers to be called a perspirational speaker rather than a motivational speaker. His tagline is 'Discuss the undiscussables to bridge the knowing-doing gaps of life'.

Yadhav earned his MBA from the Faculty of Management Studies, Delhi, India. His training & coaching firm, C-Cube Training and Development, established in 1997, has benefitted over 50,000 people across 40 nations in critical behavioural skills and competencies. His expertise and experience in observing, experimenting, and analysing behavioural patterns have helped him create implementable strategies which offer unique insights into human behaviour.

When he's not changing lives, Yadhav can be seen spending time with his dogs or playing a game of tennis.

He combines his love for the outdoors with his interest in Indian philosophy and pursuit of intelligent innocence. He believes that his treks combined with audio books provide him with most of his inspiration. Yadhav's workshops connect with people across all ages and demographics as they evolve from his own experience, his life journey from growing up in a small town to living in Gurugram, India.